Contents

D0898997

Family Desserts

Here are desserts to make any family meal special. They all start with Jell-O® gelatin, with quick and easy extras added to make just the kind of desserts you look for — perfect toppers for family meals.

Fruit Sparkle

1 package (3 oz.) Jell-O brand gelatin, any flavor

1 cup boiling water

1 bottle (7 fl. oz.) ginger ale or lemon-lime carbonated beverage, chilled

Diced or sliced drained canned or fresh fruit

Dissolve gelatin in boiling water. Add carbonated beverage and chill until thickened. Add fruit and pour into serving bowl or individual dessert dishes. Chill until set, about 1 hour. Garnish with whipped topping and fruit, if desired. Makes about 2-1/2 cups or 5 servings.

Suggested combinations:
- Raspberry flavor gelatin with 1 can (8-3/4 oz.) sliced peaches
- Lime flavor gelatin with 1 can (8-3/4 oz.) pear halves, sliced
- Cherry flavor gelatin with 1 medium banana, sliced
- Orange flavor gelatin with 1 can (8 oz.) crushed pineapple in juice
- Lemon flavor gelatin with 1 can (11 oz.) mandarin oranges

Make It Special

Rainbow in a Cloud

1 package (3 oz.) Jell-O brand gelatin, any flavor

1 cup boiling water

1/2 cup cold water

1 container (4 oz.) Cool Whip non-dairy whipped topping, thawed

Dissolve gelatin in boiling water. Add cold water and pour into 8-inch square pan. Chill until firm, at least 3 hours. Cut into cubes. Spoon about 1/3 cup of the topping into each of 6 dessert glasses. Using back of spoon, make a depression in center of each and spread topping up side of glass. Spoon gelatin cubes into topping-lined glasses and chill. Makes 6 servings.

Gelatin Specials

1 package (3 oz.) Jell-O brand gelatin, any flavor

1 cup boiling water

1 cup cold water

Dissolve gelatin in boiling water. Add cold water and proceed as directed for specific recipes.

Gelatin Parfait:
Chill gelatin mixture until set. Layer in parfait glasses with whipped topping. Garnish with fruit, if desired. Makes about 5 servings.

Fruited Gelatin:
Arrange drained canned fruit in sherbet glasses. Pour gelatin mixture over fruit and chill until firm. Garnish with whipped topping, if desired. Makes 4 servings.

Clear and Whipped Gelatin:
Chill gelatin mixture until slightly thickened. Measure 1-1/2 cups and set aside. Whip remaining gelatin with rotary beater or electric mixer until fluffy and thick. Spoon clear and whipped gelatin alternately into dessert glasses. Chill until set. Garnish with fresh fruit or whipped topping, if desired. Makes 4 servings.

Melon Wedge Coolers

1 honeydew melon (about 5 lb.)

1 package (3 oz.) Jell-O brand gelatin, any flavor

1 cup boiling water

2 cups ice cubes

1 banana, sliced

Cut melon in half lengthwise; scoop out seeds and drain well. Dissolve gelatin in boiling water. Add ice cubes and stir until gelatin begins to thicken, about 3 minutes. Remove any unmelted ice and add banana. Place melon halves in small bowls and spoon in gelatin mixture. Chill until firm, about 3 hours. (Chill any excess fruited gelatin in a dessert dish.) Cut in wedges. Makes 6 servings.

Fruit Delight

1 can (8-3/4 oz.) fruit cocktail or sliced peaches or
pear halves, diced

1 package (3 oz.) Jell-O brand gelatin, any flavor

1-1/2 cups crushed ice

Drain fruit, measuring syrup. Add water to syrup to make 3/4 cup.
Bring to a boil. Combine gelatin and boiling liquid in electric blender
container. Cover and blend on low speed until gelatin is dissolved,
about 1 minute. Add crushed ice and blend at high speed until ice is
melted, about 30 seconds. Pour into individual dessert dishes. Spoon
fruit into each dish. Chill until set, about 10 minutes. Makes 6 servings.

Speedy Ice Cream Dessert

1 package (3 oz.) Jell-O brand gelatin, any flavor

3/4 cup boiling water

1 cup vanilla ice cream

1/2 cup crushed ice

Combine gelatin and boiling water in electric blender container. Cover
and blend at low speed until gelatin is dissolved, about 1 minute. Add
ice cream and crushed ice. Blend at high speed until the ice is melted,
about 30 seconds. Pour mixture into individual dessert dishes and chill
until soft-set, about 5 minutes; or pour into a serving bowl and chill
20 minutes. Makes 2-1/2 cups or 4 servings.

Quick Jellied Ambrosia

1 package (3 oz.) Jell-O brand gelatin, orange flavor

1 cup boiling water

2 cups ice cubes

1 container (4 oz.) Cool Whip non-dairy whipped topping,
thawed

1/2 cup Baker's Angel Flake coconut

1 orange, sectioned and diced

Dissolve gelatin in boiling water. Add ice cubes and stir until gelatin
begins to thicken, 3 to 5 minutes. Remove any unmelted ice. Measure
1/2 cup gelatin and blend into whipped topping. Stir in coconut and
spoon into individual dessert dishes, making a depression in the center.
Stir orange sections into remaining gelatin and spoon into glasses.
Chill until set, about 30 minutes. Makes about 5 cups or 10 servings.

Quick Fruited Dessert

    1 package (3 oz.) Jell-O brand gelatin, any flavor

1-1/4 cups boiling water

    1 package (10 oz.) Birds Eye quick thaw fruit, any variety

Dissolve gelatin in boiling water. Add frozen fruit and stir gently until fruit thaws and separates and gelatin begins to thicken. Chill. Gelatin will be soft-set and ready to eat in about 30 minutes, or set but not firm in about 1 hour. Garnish with whipped topping, if desired. Makes about 3 cups or 6 servings.

Note: Recipe may be doubled.

Marvelous Fruit Mix-Up

| 1 package (3 oz.) Jell-O brand gelatin, any flavor |
| 3/4 cup boiling water |
| 2 cups ice cubes |
| 1 cup thawed Cool Whip non-dairy whipped topping or sour cream |
| 1 can (11 oz.) mandarin orange sections, drained |
| 1 cup miniature marshmallows |
| 1/4 cup chopped walnuts |
| 1 can (15-1/2 oz.) crushed pineapple in syrup, drained |

Dissolve gelatin in boiling water. Add ice cubes and stir constantly until gelatin starts to thicken, 3 to 5 minutes. Remove any unmelted ice. Add whipped topping, blending until smooth. Stir in mandarin oranges, marshmallows, walnuts and pineapple, reserving some fruit for garnish, if desired. Pour into serving bowl or individual dessert glasses. Chill until set. Garnish with reserved fruit. Makes 4 cups or 8 servings.

Cherry-Cola Dessert

1 can (17 oz.) pitted dark sweet cherries

1 package (3 oz.) Jell-O brand gelatin, cherry flavor

1 cup cola beverage

Drain cherries, reserving syrup. Add water to syrup to make 1 cup
and bring to a boil. Dissolve gelatin in measured liquid. Add cola
beverage and chill until slightly thickened. Add cherries and pour
into individual dessert dishes. Chill until firm, about 3 hours. Garnish
with whipped topping, if desired. Makes 3-1/4 cups or 6 servings.

Apple Whip

1 package (3 oz.) Jell-O brand gelatin, orange, lime, lemon
or raspberry flavor

1 cup boiling water

2/3 cup cold water

1-1/2 cups applesauce

1/2 teaspoon cinnamon

Dissolve gelatin in boiling water. Add cold water and chill until thickened. Beat with rotary beater or electric mixer until fluffy and thick and
about double in volume. Fold in applesauce and cinnamon. Spoon into
individual molds or 8-inch square pan. Chill until firm, at least 2 hours.
Unmold or cut in squares. Garnish with whipped topping, if desired.
Makes 5 cups or 6 to 8 servings.

Cardinal Pear Mold

1 can (8-3/4 oz.) pear halves

1 package (3 oz.) Jell-O brand gelatin, cherry flavor

1 cup boiling water

1/2 teaspoon grated orange rind (optional)

1/8 teaspoon ginger

Drain pears, reserving syrup. Add water to syrup to make 3/4 cup.
Dissolve gelatin in boiling water. Add measured liquid, grated rind
and ginger. Pour into individual molds and chill until firm, about 4 hours.
Unmold; garnish with pear halves. Makes about 2 cups or 4 servings.

Melon Bubble

1 package (3 oz.) Jell-O brand gelatin, lime, lemon or orange flavor

1 cup boiling water

1 cup cold water*

1 cup melon balls

*Or use 3/4 cup cold water and 1/4 cup orange juice

Dissolve gelatin in boiling water. Add cold water. Measure 1-1/3 cups and chill until thickened. Fold in melon balls and spoon into 6 individual dessert glasses or a serving bowl. Chill until set but not firm. Chill remaining gelatin until very thick. Whip with rotary beater or electric mixer until fluffy and thick and about double in volume. Pour over clear gelatin in glasses. Chill until firm, about 3 hours. Garnish with additional melon balls, if desired. Makes 3-1/2 cups or 6 servings.

Orange Parfait

1 package (3 oz.) Jell-O brand gelatin, orange flavor

1 cup boiling water

2 cups ice cubes

1/2 cup orange sections

1/2 cup chopped apple or sliced strawberries

1/2 cup thawed Cool Whip non-dairy whipped topping

Dissolve gelatin in boiling water. Add ice cubes and stir constantly until gelatin starts to thicken, 3 to 5 minutes. Remove any unmelted ice. Layer gelatin in parfait glasses with fruit and whipped topping, beginning and ending with gelatin. Chill 1 hour. Makes 4 or 5 servings.

Fruit Refresher

1-1/2 cups fresh berries or other fruit or combination of fruit

2 tablespoons sugar

1 package (3 oz.) Jell-O brand gelatin, any flavor

1 cup boiling water

1-1/2 cups cold water

Combine fruit and sugar; let stand 10 minutes. Dissolve gelatin in boiling water. Add cold water and chill until thickened. Stir in fruit and chill. Dessert will be soft-set, not firm. Spoon into individual dessert dishes or a serving bowl and serve plain or with cream, if desired. Makes about 4 cups or 8 servings.

Peach Special

2 packages (3 oz. each) or 1 package (6 oz.) Jell-O brand gelatin, raspberry flavor

2 cups boiling water

1-1/2 cups cold water

4 peaches, peeled and cut in half or sliced

1 pint vanilla ice cream

Dissolve gelatin in boiling water. Add cold water and pour into 9-inch square pan. Chill until firm, about 3 hours. Break into small flakes with a fork and spoon into 8 individual dessert dishes, making a depression in center of each. Place 1 peach half, cut side up, in each depression. Top with spoonfuls of ice cream. Makes 8 servings.

Lemon Sour Cream Mold

1 package (3 oz.) Jell-O brand gelatin, lemon flavor
1 cup boiling water
1/2 cup half and half or light cream
1/2 teaspoon vanilla
1/2 cup sour cream

Dissolve gelatin in boiling water. Add half and half and vanilla; blend in
sour cream. (Mixture will appear slightly curdled.) Chill until slightly
thickened. Beat until mixture is smooth. Pour into 3-cup mold. Chill
until firm, about 3 hours. Unmold and serve with fruit, if desired. Makes
about 2-1/2 cups or 5 servings.

Yogurt Whip

1 package (3 oz.) Jell-O brand gelatin, strawberry or
lemon flavor

1 cup boiling water

3/4 cup cold water

1 container (8 oz.) yogurt, plain, vanilla or strawberry flavor

Dissolve gelatin in boiling water. Add cold water and chill until slightly
thickened. Add yogurt and beat with rotary beater until mixture is light
and fluffy. Pour into individual dishes. Chill until firm, about 2 hours.
Makes 4 cups or 8 servings.

Fruit Flavor Snow

1 package (3 oz.) Jell-O brand gelatin, any flavor

1 cup boiling water

2 cups ice cubes

1 egg white

Dissolve gelatin in boiling water. Add ice cubes and stir gently until
gelatin is thickened, 3 to 5 minutes. Remove any unmelted ice. Add egg
white and whip with rotary beater or electric mixer until fluffy and thick
and about double in volume. Pile lightly in individual dessert glasses.
Chill until set, about 1 hour. Makes about 5 cups or 6 servings.
Note: For egg white, use only clean egg with no cracks in shell.

Pineapple Snow:
Substitute 1 cup pineapple juice brought to a boil for boiling
water; use orange-pineapple or orange flavor gelatin.

Chocolate-Mint Delight

1 package (3 oz.) Jell-O brand gelatin, lime flavor

1 cup boiling water

2 cups (1 pt.) vanilla ice cream

1/2 teaspoon peppermint extract

1 square Baker's semi-sweet chocolate, chopped*

*Or use 1/4 cup chocolate chips

Dissolve gelatin in boiling water. Add ice cream by spoonfuls and stir
until ice cream is melted. Add extract and chocolate. Spoon into individual dishes. Chill until set, about 30 minutes. Makes 6 servings.

Raspberry Whip

1 package (3 oz.) Jell-O brand gelatin, black raspberry flavor

1 cup boiling water

1 can (13 oz.) evaporated milk

1 tablespoon lemon juice

1 teaspoon almond extract

Dissolve gelatin in boiling water in large bowl. Gradually stir in evaporated milk, then add lemon juice and extract. Chill until thickened. Beat with rotary beater or electric mixer until fluffy and thick and about double in volume. Pour into 2-quart serving bowl. Chill until set. Garnish with lemon slices and mint leaves, if desired. Makes about 7 cups or 9 servings.

Pastel Pudding Dessert

1 package (4-serving size) Jell-O brand pudding and pie filling, vanilla, coconut cream or banana cream flavor

1 package (3 oz.) Jell-O brand gelatin, any flavor

2-1/2 cups water

1 container (4 oz.) Cool Whip non-dairy whipped topping, thawed

Combine pudding mix, gelatin and water in saucepan. Cook and stir over medium heat until mixture comes to a *full* boil and is thickened and clear. Remove from heat and chill until slightly thickened. Thoroughly blend whipped topping into the chilled pudding mixture. Spoon into individual dessert glasses or a serving bowl. Chill until firm, about 4 hours. Makes about 4 cups or 8 servings.

Suggested combinations:
- Strawberry or lime flavor gelatin with vanilla pudding
- Orange-pineapple flavor gelatin with coconut cream pudding
- Strawberry-banana flavor gelatin with banana cream pudding

Basic Bavarian

1 package (3 oz.) Jell-O brand gelatin, any flavor

1 cup boiling water

1 cup cold water

1 container (4 oz.) Cool Whip non-dairy whipped topping, thawed

Dissolve gelatin in boiling water. Add cold water. Chill until slightly thickened. Blend 1-1/2 cups whipped topping into the gelatin. Pour into individual dessert dishes or 4-cup mold. Chill until firm, at least 4 hours. Garnish with remaining whipped topping and fresh or canned fruit, if desired. Makes about 3-1/2 cups or 6 servings.

Layered Bavarian

1 package (3 oz.) Jell-O brand gelatin, any flavor
1 cup boiling water
1/2 cup cold water
1 cup ice cream

Dissolve gelatin in boiling water. Measure 1/2 cup and set aside. Add cold water to remaining gelatin and chill until slightly thickened. Blend ice cream into reserved gelatin. Spoon ice cream-gelatin mixture into dessert glasses and top with clear thickened gelatin; or spoon half the ice cream-gelatin mixture into glasses, top with half the clear gelatin and repeat layers. Chill 30 minutes. Garnish with whipped topping and fruit, if desired. Makes about 2-1/2 cups or 4 or 5 servings.

Suggested flavor combinations:

- Orange or black cherry flavor gelatin with vanilla ice cream
- Lemon flavor gelatin with vanilla or chocolate chip ice cream
- Lime flavor gelatin with vanilla or mint chip ice cream
- Strawberry flavor gelatin with burnt almond, strawberry or vanilla ice cream

Apricot Bavarian

1 can (16 oz.) apricot halves

1 package (3 oz.) Jell-O brand gelatin, apricot, orange-pineapple or strawberry flavor

1 cup boiling water

1 container (4 oz.) Cool Whip non-dairy whipped topping, thawed

Drain apricots, measuring syrup. Add water to syrup, if necessary, to make 3/4 cup. Slice the apricots. Dissolve gelatin in boiling water. Add measured liquid and chill until slightly thickened. Fold whipped topping into gelatin. Add apricots and chill again, if necessary, until mixture will mound. Spoon into individual dessert dishes or a serving bowl. Chill until set. Makes 4-1/2 cups or 8 servings.

Grape Bavarian

1 package (3 oz.) Jell-O brand gelatin, lemon flavor

1 cup boiling water

1 cup purple or white grape juice

1 container (4 oz.) Cool Whip non-dairy whipped topping, thawed

Dissolve gelatin in boiling water. Add grape juice and chill until slightly thickened. Blend whipped topping into gelatin. Spoon into individual dessert glasses or 4-cup mold. Chill until firm, about 3 hours. Garnish with additional whipped topping, if desired. Makes about 3-1/2 cups or 7 servings.

Orange-Pineapple Bavarian

1 can (20 oz.) crushed pineapple

1 package (3 oz.) Jell-O brand gelatin, orange or orange-pineapple flavor

1 cup boiling water

1 container (4 oz.) Cool Whip non-dairy whipped topping, thawed

Drain pineapple, measuring juice. Add water to juice, if necessary, to make 1 cup. Dissolve gelatin in boiling water. Add measured liquid and chill until slightly thickened. Fold whipped topping into gelatin, then fold in pineapple. Chill again, if necessary, until mixture will mound. Spoon into serving bowl or individual dessert dishes. Chill until set. Makes 5 cups or 10 servings.

Fruity Sherbet

1 package (3 oz.) Jell-O brand gelatin, orange, lemon, strawberry or raspberry flavor

1/2 cup sugar

1 cup boiling water

1 cup apricot nectar

1/2 cup orange juice

1/4 cup lemon juice

2 cups milk

Dissolve gelatin and sugar in boiling water. Add nectar, fruit juices and milk. Pour into shallow pans and freeze 1 hour. Stir, then freeze until firm, stirring several times. Makes about 5 cups or 10 servings.

Frozen Fruit Yogurt

1 package (3 oz.) Jell-O brand gelatin, orange flavor*

1 cup boiling water

3/4 cup sugar

1 cup orange juice*

2 containers (8 oz. each) plain yogurt

1 container (4 oz.) Cool Whip non-dairy whipped topping, thawed

1 cup diced orange sections (optional)

Dissolve gelatin in boiling water. Add sugar and stir until completely dissolved. Add orange juice and pour into 13x9-inch metal pan. Freeze until firm, 2 to 3 hours. Spoon frozen mixture into chilled bowl and beat until smooth. Fold in yogurt and whipped topping; add oranges. Pour into metal bowl or 9-inch square pan and freeze until firm, at least 4 hours or overnight. Makes about 7-1/2 cups or 14 servings.

*Flavor variations:
• Lemon flavor gelatin and reconstituted frozen concentrate for lemonade
• Apricot flavor gelatin and apricot nectar
• Orange flavor gelatin and cranberry juice cocktail

Fruit-Flavored Freeze

1 package (3 oz.) Jell-O brand gelatin, any flavor*

1 cup boiling water

3/4 cup sugar

2 cups milk

1 container (4 oz.) Cool Whip non-dairy whipped topping, thawed

Dissolve gelatin in boiling water. Add sugar and stir until completely dissolved. Stir in milk. (Mixture will appear curdled but will be smooth when frozen.) Pour into 13x9-inch metal pan. Freeze until icy crystals form about 1 inch around edge, about 1 hour. Spoon into chilled bowl and beat until smooth. Blend in whipped topping. Return to pan and freeze until firm, about 4 hours. Scoop into individual dishes. Makes about 5-1/2 cups or 10 servings.

*Flavors used here: black raspberry, lime, peach

Cream Cheese and Pineapple Mold

1 can (8 oz.) crushed pineapple in juice
1 package (3 oz.) Jell-O brand gelatin, any flavor
1 cup boiling water
1 tablespoon lemon juice
1 package (3 oz.) cream cheese, softened
1/4 cup chopped walnuts

Drain pineapple, reserving juice. Add water to juice to make 3/4 cup. Dissolve gelatin in boiling water. Add measured liquid and lemon juice. Gradually add 1 cup of the gelatin to the cream cheese, blending well. Chill until thickened. Meanwhile, chill remaining gelatin until thickened. Fold in pineapple and pour into dessert dishes or individual molds. Chill until set but not firm. Add walnuts to cream cheese-gelatin mixture and spoon into dishes. (Layers can be reversed, if desired.) Chill until firm, about 3 hours. Serve as a dessert with whipped topping or as a salad with mayonnaise, if desired. Makes 3 cups or 6 servings.

Cider-Cranberry Molds

3/4 cup apple cider

1/4 cup water

1 package Jell-O brand gelatin, any red flavor

3/4 cup cranberry juice cocktail

Combine cider and water in saucepan and bring to a boil. Dissolve gelatin in boiling liquid. Add cranberry juice and pour into individual molds. Chill until firm, about 3 hours. Unmold and serve as dessert with whipped topping, if desired, or as side salad. Makes 1-3/4 cups or 3 to 5 servings.

Raspberry-Melon Mold

1 package (3 oz.) Jell-O brand gelatin, black raspberry flavor

1 cup boiling water

1 package (10 oz.) Birds Eye quick thaw red raspberries

1/4 cup cold water

1 tablespoon lemon juice

1 cup cantaloupe or honeydew melon balls

Dissolve gelatin in boiling water. Add frozen berries, cold water and lemon juice. Stir gently until berries separate and gelatin begins to thicken. Chill, if necessary, until thickened. Fold in melon balls. Pour into individual molds or 4-cup mold and chill until firm, about 4 hours. Unmold and serve as dessert with whipped topping or with mayonnaise as salad. Makes 3 cups or 6 servings.

Peach and Banana Mold

1 can (8-3/4 oz.) sliced peaches

1 package (3 oz.) Jell-O brand gelatin, lime flavor

1 cup boiling water

1 banana, sliced

Drain peaches, reserving syrup. Dice peaches, if desired. Add water to syrup to make 3/4 cup. Dissolve gelatin in boiling water. Add measured liquid and chill until thickened. Fold in peaches and banana. Pour into individual molds or 4-cup mold. Chill until firm, about 3 hours. Unmold and serve with whipped topping as dessert or with mayonnaise as salad. Makes about 3 cups or 6 servings.

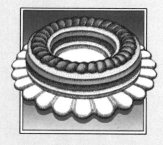

Looking for a dessert for a company dinner? A special party? The club social? Find it here. There are molds, rings, individual parfaits...some elaborate, some surprisingly easy, and all very special.

Rainbow Ribbon Mold

5 packages (3 oz. each) Jell-O brand gelatin, any 5 different flavors

6-1/4 cups boiling water

1 cup (1/2 pt.) sour cream

Dissolve one package of gelatin in 1-1/4 cups boiling water. Pour 3/4 cup into 6-cup ring mold or 9-inch square pan. Chill until set but not firm, about 15 minutes. Chill remaining gelatin in bowl; gradually blend in 3 tablespoons of the sour cream and spoon over gelatin in mold. Chill until set but not firm, about 15 minutes. Repeat with each remaining flavor of gelatin, chilling dissolved gelatin before measuring and pouring into mold. Chill at least 2 hours. Cut in wedges or rectangles. Makes about 6 cups or 12 servings.

Strawberries Romanoff

1 pint strawberries, hulled

2 tablespoons sugar

2 packages (3 oz. each) or 1 package (6 oz.) Jell-O brand gelatin, strawberry flavor

2 cups boiling water

2 tablespoons brandy*

1 tablespoon orange liqueur*

1 container (4 oz.) Cool Whip non-dairy whipped topping, thawed

*Or use 1/2 teaspoon brandy extract and 3 tablespoons orange juice.

Slice strawberries, reserving a few whole berries for garnish, if desired. Add sugar to sliced berries; let stand 15 minutes, then drain, measuring syrup. Add water to syrup to make 1 cup. Dissolve gelatin in boiling water. Measure 3/4 cup of the gelatin and add brandy, liqueur and 1/2 cup of the measured liquid. Chill until slightly thickened. Fold in whipped topping and pour into 6-cup mold. Chill until set but not firm.

Add remaining measured liquid to remaining gelatin. Chill until slightly thickened and fold in strawberries. Spoon into mold over creamy mixture. Chill until firm, at least 4 hours or overnight. Unmold and garnish with reserved berries. Makes 6 cups or 12 servings.

Jellied Peach Melba

2 packages (3 oz. each) or 1 package (6 oz.) Jell-O brand gelatin, raspberry flavor

2 cups boiling water

1/2 cup cold water

1 tablespoon lemon juice

1 package (10 oz.) Birds Eye quick thaw peaches, slightly thawed

1 package (10 oz.) Birds Eye quick thaw red raspberries, slightly thawed

1 pint vanilla ice cream

Dissolve gelatin in boiling water. Add cold water, lemon juice and the fruits. Stir gently until fruit thaws and separates and gelatin begins to thicken. Pour into 5-cup ring mold. Chill until firm, 4 hours or overnight. Unmold. Just before serving, fill center of ring with scoops of ice cream. Makes 5 cups or 8 to 10 servings.

Crown Jewel Dessert

| 1 package (3 oz.) Jell-O brand gelatin, strawberry flavor |
| 1 package (3 oz.) Jell-O brand gelatin, lemon flavor |
| 2 packages (3 oz.) Jell-O brand gelatin, orange flavor |
| 4 cups boiling water |
| 1-1/2 cups cold water |
| 1/4 cup sugar |
| 1/2 cup pineapple juice |
| 1 container (8 oz.) Cool Whip non-dairy whipped topping, thawed |

Prepare strawberry, lemon and one package of orange gelatin separately, using 1 cup boiling water and 1/2 cup cold water for each. Pour each into an 8-inch square pan. Chill until firm, about 4 hours. Cut into 1/2-inch cubes. Dissolve the remaining package of orange gelatin and sugar in 1 cup boiling water. Stir in pineapple juice and chill until slightly thickened. Blend whipped topping into gelatin. Fold in gelatin cubes and pour into 9-cup tube pan. Chill overnight or until firm. Unmold. Garnish with whipped topping, if desired. Makes 12 to 14 servings.

Charlotte Russe

2 packages (3 oz. each) Jell-O brand gelatin, black raspberry or black cherry flavor
2 cups boiling water
1 quart vanilla ice cream
12 ladyfingers, split, or thin sponge cake strips

Dissolve gelatin in boiling water. Add ice cream by spoonfuls, stirring until ice cream is completely melted. Chill until thickened. Meanwhile, trim off ends of ladyfingers and place cut ends down around sides of an 8-inch springform pan. Spoon gelatin mixture into pan and chill until firm, at least 3 hours. Remove sides of pan. Garnish with whipped topping, fruit and mint leaves, if desired. Makes about 5 cups or 10 servings.

Winter Fruit Mold

2 packages (3 oz. each) or 1 package (6 oz.) Jell-O brand gelatin, lemon flavor

2 cups boiling water

1-1/2 cups cherry wine or sherry wine

15 (about) blanched almonds, halved

1/4 teaspoon each cloves and cinnamon

1/8 teaspoon allspice

1 cup chopped candied mixed fruit

1/2 cup each light raisins and currants

1/2 cup drained maraschino or canned pitted sweet cherries, halved

1/2 cup coarsely chopped walnuts

Dissolve gelatin in boiling water. Stir in wine. Pour 1/2 cup into 6-cup ring mold. Chill until set but not firm. Arrange almonds in single layer in a decorative pattern on set gelatin. Pour another 1/2 cup of the gelatin mixture over the almonds. Chill again until set but not firm. Meanwhile, add spices, fruits and walnuts to remaining gelatin mixture; chill until thickened, then spoon gently into mold. Chill until firm, about 4 hours. Unmold and serve with whipped topping, if desired. Makes about 6 cups or 12 servings.

Cherries Supreme

1 can (16 oz.) pitted dark sweet cherries

1 package (3 oz.) Jell-O brand gelatin, any red flavor

1 cup boiling water

2 tablespoons orange juice

3/4 cup diced orange sections, well drained

1 cup thawed Cool Whip non-dairy whipped topping

1/4 cup chopped toasted almonds

Drain cherries, reserving 2/3 cup of the syrup. Dissolve gelatin in boiling water. Add reserved syrup and orange juice and chill until thickened. Fold in cherries and oranges and pour into 4-cup mold. Chill until firm, 4 hours or overnight. Combine whipped topping and toasted almonds. Unmold gelatin and serve with topping. Makes 3-1/2 cups or 6 to 8 servings.

Creamy Peach Parfait

1 package (3 oz.) cream cheese, softened

2 tablespoons sugar

1 tablespoon milk

1 package (3 oz.) Jell-O brand gelatin, peach flavor

1 cup boiling water

2 cups ice cubes

1 cup diced peeled fresh peaches

1/4 cup raspberry jam or preserves

Combine cream cheese, sugar and milk in bowl, blending well; set aside. Dissolve gelatin in boiling water. Add ice cubes and stir gently until gelatin begins to thicken, 3 to 5 minutes. Remove any unmelted ice. Fold in peaches. Spoon half the fruited gelatin into 6 parfait glasses. Carefully spoon cheese mixture into glasses over gelatin. Add a layer of preserves. Top with remaining gelatin mixture. Chill until set, about 2 hours. Garnish with whipped topping and fresh peach slices, if desired. Makes 6 servings.

Topaz Parfait

1 cup brewed Maxwell House coffee

1 package (3 oz.) Jell-O brand gelatin, lemon flavor

1/3 cup granulated sugar

1/2 cup cold water*

1/4 cup brandy or dark rum*

2 tablespoons brown sugar

1 tablespoon brandy or dark rum**

1 container (4 oz.) Cool Whip non-dairy whipped topping, thawed

*Or increase cold water to 3/4 cup and use 1 teaspoon brandy extract.

**Or use 1/2 teaspoon brandy extract.

Bring coffee to a boil. Add gelatin and granulated sugar and stir until dissolved. Add cold water and 1/4 cup brandy. Pour into 8-inch square pan. Chill until firm, about 4 hours. Cut into cubes.

Fold brown sugar and 1 tablespoon brandy into whipped topping. Layer coffee cubes and topping in parfait glasses. Makes 4 to 6 servings.

Banana-Rum Parfait

1 package (3 oz.) Jell-O brand gelatin, orange flavor

1 cup boiling water

1 cup ice cubes

1 medium banana, sliced

1 cup (1/2 pt.) vanilla ice cream

1 tablespoon light rum*

*Or use 1/4 teaspoon rum extract.

Dissolve gelatin in boiling water. Measure 1/2 cup; add ice cubes and stir constantly until gelatin starts to thicken, about 3 to 5 minutes. Remove any unmelted ice. Add banana and spoon into 5 parfait glasses. Blend ice cream and rum into remaining gelatin. Spoon over clear gelatin in glasses. Chill until set, about 30 minutes. Garnish with whipped topping, if desired. Makes 5 servings.

Art Déco Jewel

2 packages (3 oz. each) Jell-O brand gelatin, lemon flavor
2 tablespoons sugar
2 cups boiling water
1/2 cup cold water
2/3 cup orange liqueur or brandy
2 cups (1 pt.) sour cream
2 packages (3 oz. each) Jell-O brand gelatin, black cherry flavor
2 tablespoons sugar
2 cups boiling water
3/4 cup cold water

Dissolve lemon gelatin and 2 tablespoons sugar in 2 cups boiling water. Add 1/2 cup cold water and 1/3 cup liqueur. Blend in 1 cup sour cream, mixing until smooth. Place bowl of gelatin over larger bowl of ice and water and stir until slightly thickened. Pour into large glass bowl and chill until set but not firm.

Meanwhile, dissolve black cherry gelatin and 2 tablespoons sugar in 2 cups boiling water. Add 3/4 cup cold water and 1/3 cup liqueur. Chill over ice until slightly thickened. Measure 1-1/4 cups, spoon into bowl over lemon gelatin mixture and chill until set but not firm. Blend 1 cup sour cream into remaining gelatin and spoon carefully into bowl. Chill until firm, about 2 hours. Garnish with Frosted Grapes, if desired. Makes 8 cups or 16 servings.

Frosted Grapes:

Cut 2 pounds seedless green grape bunches into small clusters. Dip clusters, one at a time, into 1 beaten egg white. Hold to permit excess to drain off, then sprinkle with gelatin, using 1 package (3 oz.) Jell-O brand gelatin, any flavor. Chill on tray covered with waxed paper for about 3 hours. Use as garnish or serve as dessert.

Note: For egg white, use only clean egg, with no cracks in shell.

Patriotic Loaf

1 package (3 oz.) Jell-O brand gelatin, strawberry flavor
1 package (3 oz.) Jell-O brand gelatin, black cherry flavor
1/2 cup sugar
3 cups boiling water
1 cup cold water
1 package (3 oz.) Jell-O brand gelatin, lemon flavor
1-1/2 cups sliced fresh strawberries
1 pint vanilla ice cream
1-1/2 cups fresh, frozen or drained canned blueberries

Place strawberry and black cherry gelatin in separate bowls. Add 1/4 cup of the sugar and 1 cup of the boiling water to *each* and stir until gelatin and sugar are completely dissolved. Add 1/2 cup cold water to each mixture. Dissolve lemon gelatin in remaining 1 cup boiling water. Place bowl of strawberry gelatin mixture in larger bowl of ice and water; stir until slightly thickened and add strawberries. Pour into 9x5-inch loaf pan and chill about 5 minutes. Add ice cream to lemon gelatin, blending well. Spoon carefully into pan; chill about 5 minutes. Place bowl of black cherry gelatin mixture in larger bowl of ice and water; stir until slightly thickened. Add blueberries and spoon into pan. Chill until firm, about 6 hours or overnight. Makes 8 cups or 12 to 14 servings.

Layered Strawberry Squares

2 packages (3 oz. each) Jell-O brand gelàtin, strawberry flavor
2 cups boiling water
1 cup cold water
1 pint fresh strawberries
2 tablespoons sugar (optional)
1 container (8 oz.) Cool Whip non-dairy whipped topping, thawed
18 graham crackers

Dissolve gelatin in boiling water. Add cold water and chill until slightly thickened. Meanwhile, slice strawberries, reserving a few for garnish, if desired, and sprinkle with sugar. Fold whipped topping into gelatin, blending well; fold in strawberries. Place 9 graham crackers in bottom of 9-inch square pan. Spread half the gelatin mixture over crackers. Repeat layers. Chill until firm, about 3 hours. Cut into squares. Garnish with reserved strawberries. Makes 9 servings.

Lemon Pudding Squares

1 package (4-serving size) Jell-O brand pudding and pie filling, lemon flavor
1 package (3 oz.) Jell-O brand gelatin, lemon flavor
1/2 cup sugar
2-3/4 cups water
2 egg yolks
2 egg whites
1/4 cup sugar

Combine pudding mix, gelatin, 1/2 cup sugar and 1/4 cup of the water in a saucepan. Blend in egg yolks and add remaining water. Cook and stir over medium heat until mixture comes to a *full* boil. Remove from heat.

Beat egg whites until foamy throughout. Gradually add 1/4 cup sugar and continue beating until mixture will form stiff shiny peaks. Quickly fold in hot pudding, blending well. Pour into 8- or 9-inch square pan or individual dessert dishes. Chill at least 3 hours. Cut in squares. Serve with fresh fruit, if desired. Makes about 5-3/4 cups or 9 servings.

Fruited Chiffon Squares

2 packages (3 oz. each) Jell-O brand gelatin, orange flavor
1-1/2 cups boiling water
2 cups ice cubes
1 container (4 oz.) Cool Whip non-dairy whipped topping, thawed
1 can (8-3/4 oz.) fruit cocktail, drained

Dissolve gelatin in boiling water. Add ice cubes and stir constantly until gelatin starts to thicken, 3 to 5 minutes. Remove any unmelted ice. Measure 1 cup and fold in whipped topping, beating until smooth. Pour into 8-inch square pan and chill until set but not firm, about 5 minutes. Fold fruit into remaining gelatin and carefully spoon over creamy layer in pan. Chill until firm, at least 1 hour. Cut into squares and garnish with additional whipped topping and fruit, if desired. Makes 9 servings.

Citrus Fruit Ring

1 cup diced orange sections

1 cup diced grapefruit sections

1 package (3 oz.) Jell-O brand gelatin, orange flavor

1 cup boiling water

1 tablespoon grated orange rind

3 tablespoons chopped maraschino cherries

1/3 cup Baker's Angel Flake coconut

Drain orange and grapefruit sections, reserving juice. Add water to make 3/4 cup. Dissolve gelatin in boiling water. Add measured liquid and the orange rind and chill until thickened. Fold in orange and grapefruit sections, cherries and coconut. Pour into 4-cup ring mold or individual molds. Chill until firm, about 4 hours. Unmold and garnish with whipped topping, mint leaves, additional cherries and coconut, if desired. Makes 3-3/4 cups or 7 servings.

Brandied Cherry Ring

1 can (16 oz.) pitted dark sweet cherries

1/3 cup brandy

2 packages (3 oz. each) or 1 package (6 oz.) Jell-O brand gelatin, cherry or black cherry flavor

2 cups boiling water

1 container (4 oz.) Cool Whip non-dairy whipped topping, thawed

Drain cherries, measuring syrup; add water to syrup to make 1 cup. Cut cherries in half. Heat brandy, pour over cherries and let stand 30 minutes; drain, reserving brandy. Dissolve gelatin in boiling water. Add measured liquid and brandy and chill until thickened. Add cherries to half the gelatin and pour into 6-cup ring mold. Chill until set but not firm. Blend 1 cup whipped topping into remaining gelatin. Spoon into mold. Chill until firm, about 4 hours. Unmold and garnish with remaining whipped topping, flavored with brandy, if desired. Makes 5-1/4 cups or 10 servings.

Banana Nut Ring with Ginger Topping

| 1 can (8 oz.) crushed pineapple in juice |
| 2 packages (3 oz. each) Jell-O brand gelatin, strawberry, orange, orange-pineapple or peach flavor |
| 2 cups boiling water |
| 1/2 cup chopped pecans |
| 2 bananas, sliced |
| 1 tablespoon milk |
| 2 tablespoons slivered crystallized ginger (optional) |
| 1 container (4 oz.) Cool Whip non-dairy whipped topping, thawed |

Drain pineapple, reserving juice; add water to make 1-1/2 cups. Dissolve gelatin in boiling water. Add measured liquid and chill until thickened. Fold in pecans and bananas. Spoon into 6-cup ring mold. Chill until firm, about 4 hours.

Meanwhile, fold milk, drained pineapple and ginger into whipped topping and chill. Unmold gelatin and spoon whipped topping mixture into center. Garnish with pecan halves, banana slices and mint leaves, if desired. Makes about 5 cups or 10 servings.

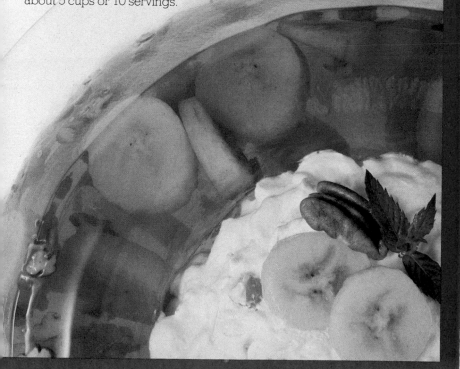

Molded Sangria

6 cups dry red wine	
3/4 cup brandy	
3 tablespoons orange liqueur	
9 whole cloves	
3 cinnamon sticks	
6 packages (3 oz. each) Jell-O brand gelatin, mixed fruit, strawberry or lemon flavor	
4-1/2 cups club soda	
3 tablespoons lime juice	
3 cups orange sections	
1-1/2 cups thinly sliced peeled apple	

Bring wine, brandy and orange liqueur to a boil with cloves and cinnamon sticks in a saucepan. Remove cinnamon sticks and cloves and pour boiling mixture over gelatin; stir until dissolved. Add club soda and lime juice and chill until thickened. Fold in orange sections and apple slices and pour into dessert glasses. Chill at least 3 hours. Garnish with whipped topping and orange slices, if desired. Makes about 3-3/4 quarts or 30 servings.

Jellied Holiday Nog

2 packages (3 oz. each) Jell-O brand gelatin, lemon flavor

2 packages (4-serving size) Jell-O brand pudding and pie filling, vanilla flavor

2 tablespoons sugar

5 cups water

1 container (8 oz.) Cool Whip non-dairy whipped topping, thawed

1/2 teaspoon rum extract

1 teaspoon vanilla

1/4 teaspoon nutmeg

Combine gelatin, pudding mix and sugar in saucepan. Add water and cook and stir over medium heat until mixture comes to a *full* boil. Remove from heat. Chill until thickened.

Thoroughly blend whipped topping, rum extract, vanilla and nutmeg into thickened pudding mixture. Pour into 8-cup mold or into large punch bowl. Chill until firm, at least 4 hours or overnight. Unmold or spoon from bowl into individual dessert glasses. Makes 16 servings.

Church Supper Special

1-1/4 cups graham cracker crumbs

1/4 cup sugar

1/4 cup butter or margarine, melted

2 packages (3 oz. each) Jell-O brand gelatin, any red flavor

2 cups boiling water

1-1/2 cups cold water

1 pound marshmallows (about 4 cups)

1 cup milk

3 medium bananas, sliced

1 container (4 oz.) Cool Whip non-dairy whipped topping, thawed

Mix crumbs, sugar and butter in 13x9-inch pan. Press onto bottom; chill. Dissolve gelatin in boiling water. Add cold water; chill until slightly thickened. Melt marshmallows in milk over low heat, stirring constantly; cool thoroughly. Arrange banana slices in a single layer on the crumb base. Blend whipped topping into the cool melted marshmallows; swirl slightly into the thickened gelatin for marbled effect. Pour over banana slices. Chill until firm. Cut into squares. Makes 20 servings.

Discover new and flavorful ways with cakes and pies, all thanks to Jell-O gelatin. Two cases in point: this Orange Coconut Cake (recipe is on page 42) and the luscious Key Lime Pie, a classic favorite.

Key Lime Pie

1 package (3 oz.) Jell-O brand gelatin, lime flavor
1 cup boiling water
1 to 2 teaspoons grated lime rind
1/2 cup lime juice
1 egg yolk, well beaten
1 can (14 oz.) sweetened condensed milk (1-1/3 cups)
1 teaspoon aromatic bitters
1 egg white
Few drops green food coloring (optional)
1 baked 9-inch pie shell, cooled

Dissolve gelatin in boiling water. Add lime rind and juice and pour slowly into beaten egg yolk, stirring constantly. Add condensed milk and bitters and chill until slightly thickened. Beat egg white until stiff peaks will form; fold into gelatin mixture. Add food coloring. Pour into pie shell. Chill until firm, about 3 hours. Garnish with whipped topping and lime slices, if desired.

Note: Use only clean egg, with no cracks in shell.

Orange Coconut Cake (shown on page 41)

1 package (3 oz.) Jell-O brand gelatin, orange flavor

1-1/3 cups (about) Baker's Angel Flake coconut

1 package (2-layer size) white cake mix or pudding-included cake mix

1 package fluffy white frosting mix

Measure 1 tablespoon of the gelatin into a jar. Add coconut; cover and shake until coconut is evenly tinted.

Prepare cake mix as directed on package, adding remaining gelatin before beating. Bake in two 9-inch layer pans which have been greased and floured and then lined on bottoms with waxed paper. Cool in pans 10 minutes. Remove from pans and finish cooling on racks. Prepare frosting mix as directed on package. Fill and frost layers with prepared frosting and sprinkle with tinted coconut. Garnish with orange slices, if desired.

In high altitude areas, follow package directions, add 3/4 cup all-purpose flour and use 1-2/3 cups water; bake at 375° for 30 minutes.

Marble Angel Cake

1 package angel food cake mix

1 package (3 oz.) Jell-O brand gelatin, any flavor

Prepare cake mix as directed on package, folding gelatin into about 1/3 of the batter. Alternately spoon batters into ungreased 10-inch tube pan. Zigzag spatula through batters to marble. Bake on lowest oven rack at 375° for 35 to 40 minutes, or until top is golden brown and springs back when lightly pressed. Turn cake upside down over funnel or bottle to cool completely. Remove from pan. Frost with whipped topping, if desired.

In high altitude areas, follow package directions.

Rosy Peach Upside-Down Cake

| 1 can (29 oz.) sliced peaches, drained* |
| 1 package (3 oz.) Jell-O brand gelatin, strawberry flavor |
| 1 package (3 oz.) Jell-O brand gelatin, peach flavor |
| 1 teaspoon cinnamon (optional) |
| 1/3 cup butter or margarine |
| 1 package (2-layer size) yellow cake mix or pudding-included cake mix |
| 1 cup thawed Cool Whip non-dairy whipped topping |

*Or use 2 cups sliced peeled fresh peaches.

Arrange peaches in buttered 13x9-inch pan. Combine strawberry and peach gelatin and cinnamon in a small bowl. Sprinkle about 3/4 of the mixture evenly over peaches and dot with butter. Prepare cake mix as directed on package. Pour 3/4 of the batter into pan. Stir remaining gelatin mixture into remaining cake batter; blend well and pour into pan. Zigzag spatula through batter to marble. Bake at 350° for 45 minutes, or until cake tester inserted in center comes out clean. Cool 5 minutes in pan, then invert onto serving platter and cool. Garnish with whipped topping.

In high altitude areas, follow package directions and bake at 350° for 45 to 50 minutes.

Christmas Rainbow Poke Cake

2 baked 8- or 9-inch white cake layers, cooled

1 package (3 oz.) Jell-O brand gelatin, raspberry flavor

1 package (3 oz.) Jell-O brand gelatin, lime flavor

2 cups boiling water

1 container (8 oz.) Cool Whip non-dairy whipped topping, thawed

Place cake layers, top sides up, in two clean 8- or 9-inch layer pans. Prick each cake with fork at 1/2-inch intervals.

Meanwhile, dissolve each package of gelatin separately in 1 cup of the boiling water. Carefully pour raspberry flavor gelatin over one cake layer and lime flavor gelatin over second cake layer. Chill 3 to 4 hours. Dip one cake pan in warm water for 10 seconds; then unmold onto serving plate and top with about 1 cup of the whipped topping. Unmold second layer carefully onto first layer. Frost top and sides with remaining topping. Chill. Garnish with Gumdrop Holly Leaves, if desired.

Gumdrop Holly Leaves:
Sprinkle pastry board with lime flavor gelatin or sugar. Flatten green gumdrops with rolling pin until about 1/16 inch thick, turning frequently to coat with gelatin. Cut flattened gumdrops into holly leaf shapes. Use red gumdrop rounds or halved candied cherries for berries.

Gelatin Poke Cake

1 package (2-layer size) white cake mix or pudding-included cake mix

1 package (3 oz.) Jell-O brand gelatin, any flavor

1 cup boiling water

1/2 cup cold water

Prepare cake batter as directed on package and pour into well-greased and floured 13x9-inch pan. Bake at 350° for 30 to 35 minutes, or until cake tester inserted in center comes out clean. Cool cake in pan 15 minutes, then prick with fork at 1/2-inch intervals. Meanwhile, dissolve gelatin in boiling water. Add cold water and carefully pour over cake. Chill 3 to 4 hours. Garnish with whipped topping, if desired.

In high altitude areas, follow package directions.

Streusel Poke Cake

1-1/2 cups graham cracker crumbs

1/2 cup chopped walnuts

1/2 teaspoon cinnamon

1/2 cup melted butter or margarine

1 package (2-layer size) yellow cake mix or pudding-included cake mix

1 package (3 oz.) Jell-O brand gelatin, strawberry flavor

1 cup boiling water

1/2 cup cold water

Combine crumbs, nuts, cinnamon and butter and set aside.

Prepare cake mix as directed on package and pour half the batter into well-greased and floured 13x9-inch pan. Sprinkle with half the crumb mixture and top with remaining batter. Bake at 350° for 35 to 40 minutes, or until cake tester inserted in center comes out clean. Cool cake in pan 15 minutes, then prick with fork at 1/2-inch intervals.

Meanwhile, dissolve gelatin in boiling water. Add cold water and carefully pour over cake. Chill 3 to 4 hours. Sprinkle with confectioners sugar, if desired.

In high altitude areas, follow package directions.

Strawberry Angel Cake

2 packages (3 oz. each) or 1 package (6 oz.) Jell-O brand gelatin, strawberry flavor

2 cups boiling water

1 cup cold water

1 pint fresh strawberries

2 tablespoons sugar (optional)

1 container (8 oz.) Cool Whip non-dairy whipped topping, thawed

1 commercial (14 oz.) angel food cake, cut into 1-inch cubes

Dissolve gelatin in boiling water. Add cold water and chill until slightly thickened. Slice strawberries, reserving a few for garnish, if desired, and sprinkle with sugar. Blend whipped topping into gelatin, then fold in strawberries and cake cubes. Spoon into 10-inch tube pan and chill until firm, about 3 hours. Unmold and garnish with additional whipped topping and reserved strawberries.

Peach Cake Squares

1 package (3 oz.) Jell-O brand gelatin, orange-pineapple or peach flavor

2 tablespoons sugar

1-1/2 cups boiling water

1 cup cold water

1 teaspoon lemon juice

1 cup sweetened sliced fresh peaches*

1 baked 8-inch square sponge cake

*Or use 1 package (10 oz.) Birds Eye quick thaw peaches, thawed and drained.

Dissolve gelatin and sugar in boiling water. Add cold water, lemon juice and peaches. Chill until slightly thickened, about 2 hours, stirring occasionally. (Or place bowl of gelatin mixture in larger bowl of ice and water; stir until slightly thickened.) Cut sponge cake into 9 squares and place in individual dessert dishes. Spoon thickened gelatin mixture over cake squares and top with whipped topping, if desired. Makes 9 servings.

Party Layer Cake

1 package (3 oz.) Jell-O brand gelatin, orange flavor*

1/2 cup boiling water

1 can (8 oz.) crushed pineapple in juice*

2 cups ice cubes

2 baked 9-inch yellow or white cake layers, cooled

1 container (8 oz.) Cool Whip non-dairy whipped topping, thawed

Thoroughly dissolve gelatin in boiling water. Add undrained pineapple and ice cubes. Stir gently until gelatin begins to thicken, 3 to 5 minutes. Remove any unmelted ice and chill until slightly thickened. Measure 1 cup and spoon over one cake layer. Chill about 10 minutes.

Meanwhile, thoroughly blend whipped topping into remaining gelatin mixture. Place second cake layer over filling and spread gelatin-topping mixture over top and sides of cake. Chill. Garnish with fruit, if desired. Store any leftover cake in refrigerator. Makes 1 cup filling and about 4 cups frosting.

*Flavor variations:
- Use strawberry, peach or raspberry flavor gelatin and 1 package (10 oz.) Birds Eye quick thaw strawberries, peaches or red raspberries. Dissolve gelatin in 1 cup boiling water, add fruit and stir gently until fruit thaws and separates and gelatin begins to thicken. Then proceed as above.

Pie Superstars

Lemon Chiffon Pie

3 egg yolks, slightly beaten

1-1/2 cups water

1/2 cup sugar

1 package (3 oz.) Jell-O brand gelatin, lemon flavor

3 tablespoons lemon juice

1-1/2 teaspoons grated lemon rind

3 egg whites

Dash of salt

1 baked 9-inch pie shell or crumb crust, cooled

Combine egg yolks and 1 cup of the water in saucepan; add 1/4 cup of the sugar. Cook and stir over low heat until mixture is slightly thickened and just comes to a boil. Remove from heat. Add gelatin and stir until dissolved. Add remaining 1/2 cup water, lemon juice and rind and chill until slightly thickened. Beat egg whites and salt until foamy throughout. Gradually beat in remaining 1/4 cup sugar and continue beating until mixture will stand in stiff peaks. Fold in thickened gelatin and blend well. Chill again, if necessary, until mixture will mound. Spoon into pie shell. Chill until firm, about 4 hours.

Note: Use only clean eggs, with no cracks in shell.

Grasshopper Pie

1 package (3 oz.) Jell-O brand gelatin, lime flavor

1 cup boiling water

1/2 cup cold water

3 tablespoons green creme de menthe liqueur

3 tablespoons white creme de cacao liqueur

1/2 teaspoon vanilla

1 egg white

2 tablespoons sugar

1 cup thawed Cool Whip non-dairy whipped topping

1 baked 9-inch pie shell or crumb crust, cooled

Dissolve gelatin in boiling water. Add cold water, liqueurs and vanilla and chill until slightly thickened. Measure 1/2 cup and set aside. Beat egg white until foamy throughout. Gradually beat in sugar and continue beating until mixture will form stiff shiny peaks. Thoroughly blend egg white mixture and whipped topping into remaining gelatin mixture.

Pour about half the creamy gelatin mixture into the pie shell; drizzle with half the reserved clear gelatin. Repeat layers and zigzag spatula through filling to marble. Chill until firm, about 3 hours.

Note: For egg white, use clean egg with no cracks in shell.

Strawberry Bavarian Pie

| 1 package (3 oz.) Jell-O brand gelatin, strawberry flavor |
| 1/4 cup sugar |
| 1 cup boiling water |
| 1/4 cup cold water |
| 1 pint strawberries, hulled and halved |
| 1 baked 9-inch pie shell, cooled |
| 1 container (4 oz.) Cool Whip non-dairy whipped topping, thawed |

Dissolve gelatin and sugar in boiling water. Add cold water and chill until thickened.

Meanwhile, arrange strawberries in bottom of pie shell. Beat thickened gelatin with electric mixer or rotary beater until fluffy and thick and about double in volume. Blend in 1 cup of the whipped topping. Chill again, if necessary, until mixture will mound. Spoon into shell over berries. Chill about 4 hours. Garnish with remaining whipped topping and additional berries, if desired.

Fresh Fruit Pie

1 package (3 oz.) Jell-O brand gelatin, any flavor

1 cup boiling water

2 cups ice cubes

Fresh fruit

1 baked 8-inch pie shell, cooled

Dissolve gelatin in boiling water. Add ice cubes and stir constantly until gelatin begins to thicken, about 3 to 5 minutes. Remove any unmelted ice. Add fruit and spoon into pie shell. Chill until firm, about 3 hours. Garnish with whipped topping, if desired.

Fruit-gelatin combinations:
- 1 banana, sliced, with raspberry, lime or orange flavor gelatin
- 3 fresh peaches, peeled and sliced (about 2 cups), and 1/2 teaspoon almond extract with orange or peach flavor gelatin
- 1 pint strawberries, sliced, with strawberry flavor gelatin

Avocado Lime Pie

1 can (8-3/4 oz.) crushed pineapple in syrup

2 tablespoons lemon or lime juice

1 package (3 oz.) Jell-O brand gelatin, lime flavor

1/4 teaspoon salt

1 cup boiling water

1 ripe medium avocado, peeled and halved

1 package (3 oz.) cream cheese, softened

1 cup thawed Cool Whip non-dairy whipped topping

1 baked 9-inch graham cracker crumb crust, cooled

Drain pineapple, reserving syrup. Add lemon juice to syrup, then add water to make 3/4 cup. Dissolve gelatin and salt in boiling water. Add measured liquid and chill until slightly thickened.

Meanwhile, dice half of the avocado. Place remaining avocado and the cream cheese in electric blender container and blend until smooth. Fold cheese mixture, diced avocado, pineapple and whipped topping into the thickened gelatin. Spoon into crust. Chill until firm, at least 3 hours. Garnish with additional whipped topping, if desired.

Jellied Fruit Tarts

1 package (3 oz.) Jell-O brand gelatin, orange flavor
1 cup boiling water
1 package (10 oz.) Birds Eye quick thaw strawberries
1 can (11 oz.) mandarin orange sections, drained
1 small banana, sliced
8 baked 3-inch tart shells, cooled*

*Or use 1 baked 8- or 9-inch graham cracker crumb crust, cooled.

Dissolve gelatin in boiling water. Add frozen strawberries and stir until fruit thaws and separates. Fold in oranges and banana. Spoon into tart shells. Chill at least 2 hours. Garnish with whipped topping and fruit, if desired.

Light 'n Fruity Pie

1 package (3 oz.) Jell-O brand gelatin, any flavor

2/3 cup boiling water

2 cups ice cubes

1 container (8 oz.) Cool Whip non-dairy whipped topping, thawed

1 baked 8- or 9-inch graham cracker crumb crust, cooled

Dissolve gelatin completely in boiling water, stirring 3 minutes. Add ice cubes and stir constantly until gelatin is thickened, about 2 to 3 minutes. Remove any unmelted ice. Using wire whip, blend in whipped topping and whip until smooth. Chill, if necessary, until mixture will mound. Spoon into pie crust. Chill 2 hours. Garnish with fruit, if desired.

Fruited version:
Make as directed above, folding 1 cup fresh or canned fruit, drained and sliced, into gelatin-topping mixture before chilling; use 9-inch crumb crust. Garnish with additional fruit, if desired.

Blender Cheese Pie

1 package (3 oz.) Jell-O brand gelatin, any flavor

1 cup boiling water

1 package (3 oz.) cream cheese, cut into small pieces

1 cup crushed ice or ice cubes

1 container (4 oz.) Cool Whip non-dairy whipped topping, thawed

1 baked 8- or 9-inch graham cracker crumb crust, cooled

Combine gelatin and boiling water in electric blender container. Cover and blend at low speed until gelatin is dissolved, about 1 minute. Add cream cheese; cover and blend at low speed for 30 seconds. Add ice and whipped topping; cover and blend at high speed until ice is melted, about 30 seconds. Pour into crust and chill at least 2 hours.

Yogurt Pie

1 package (3 oz.) Jell-O brand gelatin, any flavor

3/4 cup boiling water

2 containers (8 oz. each) plain or fruit-flavored yogurt

1 8-inch graham cracker crumb crust

Dissolve gelatin completely in boiling water, stirring about 3 minutes. Chill until slightly thickened. Using wire whip, gradually add gelatin to yogurt in a bowl, beating until smooth. Chill again, if necessary, until mixture will mound. Spoon into crust and chill until firm, about 4 hours.

Super Ice Cream Pie

1 package (3 oz.) Jell-O brand gelatin, any flavor

2/3 cup boiling water

1 pint ice cream, any flavor

1 container (4 oz.) Cool Whip non-dairy whipped topping, thawed

1 baked 8- or 9-inch graham cracker crumb crust, cooled

Dissolve gelatin in boiling water. Add ice cream by spoonfuls, stirring until melted and smooth. Blend in whipped topping and chill, if necessary, until mixture will mound. Spoon into pie crust. Chill at least 2 hours or freeze until firm, about 3 hours.

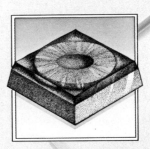

Gelatin side salads have a way of making everyday dinners special. They're easy, too. For help in choosing just the right salad to perk up your dinner entree, turn to The Family Salad Selector, page 73.

Creamy Fruit Salad

1 can (about 8 oz.) fruit

2 packages (3 oz. each) Jell-O brand gelatin, lime, lemon, apricot or orange flavor

1-3/4 cups boiling water

1/2 cup sour cream or plain yogurt

3/4 cup cold water

1 tablespoon lemon juice

Drain fruit, reserving 2/3 cup syrup. Dissolve 1 package gelatin in 3/4 cup of the boiling water. Add measured syrup. Blend in sour cream, beating until smooth. Chill until slightly thickened. Pour into 8-inch square pan and chill until set but not firm. Dissolve remaining gelatin in remaining boiling water. Add cold water and lemon juice and chill until slightly thickened. Arrange fruit on creamy layer in pan. Spoon clear gelatin over fruit. Chill until firm, about 4 hours. Cut into squares. Makes 9 servings.

Flavor suggestions:
• Lime flavor gelatin with 1 can (8 oz.) sliced pineapple in juice
• Lemon flavor gelatin with 1 can (8-3/4 oz.) sliced peaches
• Apricot flavor gelatin with 1 can (8-3/4 oz.) apricot halves

Quick Waldorf Salad

| 1 package (3 oz.) Jell-O brand gelatin, orange flavor |
| 3/4 cup boiling water |
| 1-1/2 cups crushed ice |
| 1 tablespoon lemon juice |
| 3/4 cup diced unpeeled apple |
| 1/4 cup chopped celery |
| 1/4 cup chopped nuts |

Combine gelatin and boiling water in electric blender container. Blend at low speed until gelatin is dissolved, about 1 minute. Add ice and lemon juice; cover and blend at high speed until ice is melted, about 30 seconds. Stir in apple, celery and nuts. Pour into 8x4-inch loaf pan or 4-cup mold. Chill until firm, about 2 hours. Unmold. Garnish with apple slices and nut halves, if desired. Makes about 4 cups or 8 servings.

Speedy Sunset Salad

1 can (8 oz.) crushed pineapple in juice

1 package (3 oz.) Jell-O brand gelatin, lemon flavor

1/2 teaspoon salt

1-1/2 cups crushed ice

1 tablespoon lemon juice or vinegar

1 cup grated carrots

Drain pineapple, reserving juice. Add water to juice to make 3/4 cup and bring to a boil. Combine measured liquid, gelatin and salt in electric blender container. Cover and blend at low speed until gelatin is dissolved, about 1 minute. Add ice and lemon juice; cover and blend at high speed until ice is melted. Add pineapple and carrots and pour into 4-cup mold or individual molds. Chill until firm, about 2 hours. Unmold. Makes 4 cups or 8 servings.

Self-Layering Salad

1 can (8-3/4 oz.) sliced peaches, drained and diced

1/4 cup sliced celery

1 package (3 oz.) Jell-O brand gelatin, lemon, orange or lime flavor

3/4 cup boiling water

1-1/2 cups crushed ice

Place peaches and celery in 9x5-inch loaf pan. Combine gelatin and boiling water in electric blender container. Cover and blend at low speed until gelatin is dissolved, about 1 minute. Add crushed ice and blend at high speed until ice is melted, about 30 seconds. Pour over peaches and celery in pan. Chill until firm, about 2 hours. Unmold. Makes about 4 cups or 8 servings.

Mixed Vegetable Salad

2 packages (3 oz. each) or 1 package (6 oz.) Jell-O brand gelatin, lemon flavor

2 beef bouillon cubes

2 cups boiling water

1 package (10 oz.) Birds Eye 5 minute mixed vegetables

1-1/4 cups cold water

2 tablespoons vinegar

Dissolve gelatin and bouillon cubes in boiling water. Add frozen vegetables and stir until vegetables separate and gelatin begins to thicken. Stir in cold water and vinegar. Pour into individual molds or 5-cup mold. Chill until firm, about 2 hours. Unmold. Makes 4-3/4 cups or 9 servings.

Spinach-Cottage Cheese Salad

1 package (10 oz.) Birds Eye 5 minute chopped spinach

1 package (3 oz.) Jell-O brand gelatin, lemon flavor

1 cup boiling water

2 teaspoons Worcestershire sauce

1/2 cup mayonnaise

1/2 cup cottage cheese

Thaw frozen spinach for 15 minutes; cut into small cubes. Dissolve gelatin in boiling water. Add spinach and stir until spinach separates and gelatin begins to thicken. Blend in Worcestershire sauce, mayonnaise and cottage cheese. Pour into 4-cup mold and chill until firm, about 2 hours. Unmold. Makes 4 cups or 8 servings.

Broccoli-Yogurt Salad

1 package (3 oz.) Jell-O brand gelatin, lemon flavor

1/2 teaspoon salt

3/4 cup boiling water

1 package (10 oz.) Birds Eye 5 minute chopped broccoli, cut in small cubes

1 container (8 oz.) plain yogurt

2 teaspoons minced onion

Dissolve gelatin and salt in boiling water. Add frozen broccoli and stir until broccoli separates and gelatin begins to thicken. Blend in yogurt and add onion. Pour into 4-cup mold. Chill until firm, about 2 hours. Unmold. Makes 3-2/3 cups or 7 servings.

French Bean Basket

2 packages (3 oz. each) or 1 package (6 oz.) Jell-O brand gelatin, lemon flavor

2 chicken bouillon cubes

2 cups boiling water

1 package (9 oz.) Birds Eye 5 minute French style green beans

1-1/4 cups cold water

1 tablespoon lemon juice

2 tablespoons chopped pimiento

Dissolve gelatin and bouillon cubes in boiling water. Add frozen beans and stir until beans separate and gelatin begins to thicken. Stir in cold water, lemon juice and pimiento. Pour into 4- or 5-cup ring mold or individual molds. Chill until firm, about 2 hours. Unmold and garnish with crisp greens, if desired. Makes about 4 cups or 8 servings.

Yogurt Garden Salad

1 package (3 oz.) Jell-O brand gelatin, lemon flavor

1/2 teaspoon salt

1 cup boiling water

1 tablespoon vinegar

1 container (8 oz.) plain yogurt

1 cup grated carrots

1/2 cup chopped green pepper

1 tablespoon chopped chives

Dissolve gelatin and salt in boiling water. Add vinegar and chill until slightly thickened. Blend in yogurt, then fold in carrots, green pepper and chives. Pour into 2-1/2- or 3-cup mold. Chill until firm, about 3 hours. Unmold. Makes 2-1/2 cups or 5 servings.

Pineapple-Cottage Cheese Salad

1 package (3 oz.) Jell-O brand gelatin, apricot or peach flavor

1 container (16 oz.) creamed cottage cheese

1 cup shredded carrots

1 can (8-1/4 oz.) crushed pineapple in syrup

1 cup thawed Cool Whip non-dairy whipped topping

1/2 cup mayonnaise

Add gelatin right from the pouch to cottage cheese and blend well. Stir in carrots, pineapple, whipped topping and mayonnaise, mixing well. Chill at least 1 hour. Scoop or spoon onto lettuce leaves. Makes 4-1/2 cups or 8 servings.

Cranberry-Sour Cream Mold

1 package (3 oz.) Jell-O brand gelatin, any red flavor

1 cup boiling water

1 can (8 oz.) whole berry or jellied cranberry sauce

1 teaspoon grated orange rind (optional)

1/2 cup sour cream

Dissolve gelatin in boiling water. Break up cranberry sauce with a fork. Blend cranberry sauce and orange rind into gelatin. Fold in sour cream. Pour into 3-cup mold or individual molds. Chill until firm. Unmold. Makes 2-1/2 cups or 4 or 5 servings.

Fruit and Cream Cheese Salad

1 can (16 oz.) fruit cocktail in juice
2 packages (3 oz. each) or 1 package (6 oz.) Jell-O brand gelatin, strawberry flavor
2 cups boiling water
2 packages (3 oz. each) cream cheese, softened
1/4 teaspoon cinnamon

Drain fruit cocktail, reserving juice. Add water to juice to make 1 cup. Dissolve gelatin in boiling water. Add measured liquid. Measure 2-1/4 cups of the mixture and chill until thickened. Blend remaining gelatin slowly into cream cheese and cinnamon, beating until smooth; set aside. Add fruit cocktail to thickened gelatin and pour into 6-cup fluted tube pan or mold or 10 individual molds. Chill until set but not firm, about 15 minutes. Top with cream cheese-gelatin mixture. Chill until firm, about 3 hours. Unmold. Makes about 5-1/3 cups or 10 servings.

Florida Sunshine Salad

1/2 cup fresh orange sections, halved

1/2 cup grapefruit sections, halved

1 tablespoon sugar

1 package (3 oz.) Jell-O brand gelatin, lemon or orange flavor

1 cup boiling water

Sprinkle fruit with sugar; let stand 10 to 15 minutes. Drain, measuring juice, and add water to make 3/4 cup. Dissolve gelatin in boiling water; add measured liquid. Measure 3/4 cup gelatin into bowl and set aside. Chill remaining gelatin until thickened. Fold in fruit and pour into serving bowl. Chill until set but not firm. Place bowl of measured gelatin in larger bowl of ice and water. Stir until slightly thickened, then whip with electric mixer or rotary beater until fluffy and thick and about double in volume. Pour into bowl over clear gelatin and chill until firm, about 3 hours. Garnish with additional fruit and mint leaves, if desired. Makes about 4 cups or 6 servings.

Melon Salad

2 packages (3 oz. each) Jell-O brand gelatin, peach or apricot flavor

2 cups boiling water

1 cup cold water

3/4 cup mayonnaise

1 cup (about) halved melon balls

Dissolve gelatin in boiling water; add cold water. Measure 1-1/2 cups gelatin and blend in mayonnaise. Pour into 8-inch square pan and chill until set but not firm. Chill remaining gelatin until slightly thickened. Arrange melon balls on mayonnaise-gelatin layer and top with clear gelatin. Chill until firm, about 3 hours. Cut into squares. Garnish with crisp greens, melon balls and mint sprigs, if desired. Makes 9 servings.

Strawberry-Banana Squares

2 packages (3 oz. each) or 1 package (6 oz.) Jell-O brand gelatin, lime or strawberry flavor

2 cups boiling water

1-1/4 cups cold water

1 package (8 oz.) cream cheese, softened

1/2 cup sliced strawberries

1/2 cup sliced banana

Dissolve gelatin in boiling water. Add cold water. Measure 1-3/4 cups and set aside. Gradually blend remaining gelatin into cream cheese. Pour into 8-inch square pan. Chill until set but not firm. Meanwhile, chill measured gelatin until slightly thickened. Fold in strawberries and banana and spoon into pan. Chill until firm, about 3 hours. Cut into squares. Makes 9 servings.

Garden Salad

1 package (3 oz.) Jell-O brand gelatin, lemon flavor
1/2 teaspoon salt
1 cup boiling water
3/4 cup cold water
1 tablespoon vinegar
Vegetable combination*

Dissolve gelatin and salt in boiling water. Add cold water and vinegar and chill until slightly thickened. Add vegetable combination and pour into individual molds. Chill until firm, about 3 hours. Unmold and garnish with crisp salad greens, if desired. Makes about 2 cups or 4 servings.

*Vegetable combinations:
- 1/2 cup raw cauliflower pieces and 2 tablespoons diced pimiento
- 1/4 cup sliced celery, 1/4 cup chopped green pepper and 1/4 cup sliced olives

- 1/2 cup sliced radishes and 1 tablespoon sliced scallions
- 1 small tomato, cut in thin wedges, 1/4 cup sliced celery or radishes and 1/4 cup quartered cucumber slices
- 1 cup shredded carrots, 1/2 cup diced celery and 1/4 cup sliced green olives

Zucchini Salad

1 package (3 oz.) Jell-O brand gelatin, lemon flavor

1/8 teaspoon salt

1 cup boiling water

3/4 cup cold water

1 tablespoon lemon juice

2 medium zucchini, shredded (1-1/2 cups)

1 tablespoon grated onion

1 tablespoon chopped pimiento

Dissolve gelatin and salt in boiling water. Add cold water and lemon juice and chill until thickened. Fold in zucchini, onion and pimiento and pour into 3-cup mold. Chill until firm, about 4 hours. Unmold. Makes 2-3/4 cups or 5 servings.

Cucumber-Sour Cream Mold

2 cucumbers, peeled and coarsely grated (1-1/2 cups)

1 package (3 oz.) Jell-O brand gelatin, lemon or lime flavor

1/2 teaspoon salt

1 cup boiling water

1/2 cup cold water

2 teaspoons vinegar

1/2 cup sour cream

1 tablespoon chopped onion

1 tablespoon chopped parsley

1/8 teaspoon coarsely ground black pepper

Wrap grated cucumbers in a clean cloth and squeeze tightly to remove liquid; drain. Dissolve gelatin and salt in boiling water. Add cold water and vinegar. Blend in sour cream and chill until thickened. Fold in drained cucumbers, onion, parsley and pepper. Pour into individual molds or 4-cup mold. Chill until firm, about 4 hours. Unmold. Makes about 3-2/3 cups or 7 servings.

Fruit Cocktail Salad

1 can (8-3/4 oz.) fruit cocktail

1 package (3 oz.) Jell-O brand gelatin, any red flavor

1/2 teaspoon salt

1 cup boiling water

1 tablespoon lemon juice

1 cup (8 oz.) cottage cheese

Drain fruit, measuring syrup. Add water to syrup to make 3/4 cup. Dissolve gelatin and salt in boiling water. Add measured liquid and lemon juice. Chill until slightly thickened. Add cottage cheese and fruit cocktail. Pour into 4-cup mold or individual molds. Chill until firm, about 3 hours. Unmold. Makes 4 cups or 8 servings.

Cranberry-Orange Salad

1 package (3 oz.) Jell-O brand gelatin, any red flavor

1/8 teaspoon salt

3/4 cup boiling water

1/8 teaspoon cinnamon

Dash of cloves

1 can (8 oz.) whole berry cranberry sauce

1 tablespoon grated orange rind (optional)

1 cup diced orange sections

Dissolve gelatin and salt in boiling water; add spices. Add cranberry sauce and orange rind. Chill until thickened. Fold in oranges and pour into 3-cup mold or individual molds. Chill until firm, about 3 hours. Unmold. Makes about 2-1/4 cups or 4 servings.

Spiced Peaches

1 can (17 oz.) sliced peaches

1/4 cup vinegar

1/2 cup sugar

12 whole cloves

1 cinnamon stick

1 package (3 oz.) Jell-O brand gelatin, orange flavor

3/4 cup cold water

67

Drain peaches, reserving 3/4 cup syrup. Combine syrup, vinegar, sugar and spices in saucepan. Bring to a boil, add peaches and simmer 10 minutes. Strain syrup; add boiling water to make 1 cup. Place peaches in individual molds or 3-cup mold. Dissolve gelatin in measured liquid. Add cold water and pour over peaches in molds. Chill until firm, about 3 hours. Unmold. Makes 2-1/2 cups or 5 servings.

Frozen Fruit Salad

1 can (11 oz.) mandarin orange sections

1 package (3 oz.) Jell-O brand gelatin, lime flavor

1 cup boiling water

1 cup (1/2 pt.) sour cream

1/2 cup mayonnaise

1 cup miniature marshmallows

1/4 cup chopped nuts

Drain orange sections, reserving syrup. Add water to syrup to make 1/2 cup. Dissolve gelatin in boiling water. Add measured liquid and chill until slightly thickened. Blend sour cream and mayonnaise into gelatin; chill again until thickened. Fold in orange sections, marshmallows and nuts. Spoon into 8-inch square pan or 8x4-inch loaf pan and freeze until firm. Unmold and garnish with crisp salad greens and additional fruit, if desired. Makes 5 cups or 10 servings.

Tomato Aspic

1 package (3 oz.) Jell-O brand gelatin, lemon flavor

1 teaspoon salt

1 cup boiling tomato juice

2/3 cup cold tomato juice

1 tablespoon lemon juice

1 teaspoon prepared horseradish

1/2 teaspoon grated onion

Dissolve gelatin and salt in boiling tomato juice. Add cold juice, lemon juice, horseradish and onion and pour into 8x4- or 9x5-inch loaf pan. Chill until firm, about 4 hours. Cut into squares. Makes 4 servings.

Zesty Spring Salad

1 package (3 oz.) Jell-O brand gelatin, lemon flavor

1/2 teaspoon salt

1 cup boiling water

1/2 cup cold water

1 tablespoon steak sauce

2 teaspoons vinegar

2/3 cup diced seeded tomato

2 tablespoons chopped scallions or onions

Dissolve gelatin and salt in boiling water. Add cold water, steak sauce and vinegar and chill until slightly thickened. Fold in tomato and scallions and pour into 2-1/2- or 3-cup mold. Chill until firm, about 3 hours. Unmold. Makes about 3 cups or 6 servings.

Molded Beet Salad

1 can (16 oz.) sliced beets

1/2 cup tomato juice

1 package (3 oz.) Jell-O brand gelatin, lemon flavor

1/2 teaspoon salt

1 teaspoon vinegar

1 container (8 oz.) plain yogurt

Drain beets, reserving 1/2 cup liquid. Chop beets and set aside. Bring measured liquid and tomato juice to a boil; remove from heat. Dissolve gelatin and salt in hot liquid. Add vinegar and chill until slightly thickened. Blend in yogurt, then fold in beets. Pour into 3-cup mold or individual molds. Chill until firm. Unmold. Makes 6 servings.

Barbecue Cottage Cheese Salad

1 package (3 oz.) Jell-O brand gelatin, lemon, orange or orange-pineapple flavor

1/2 teaspoon salt

3/4 cup boiling water

1 can (8 oz.) tomato sauce

1 tablespoon vinegar

Dash of pepper

Cottage cheese

Dissolve gelatin and salt in boiling water. Blend in tomato sauce, vinegar and pepper. Pour into individual ring molds and chill until firm, about 4 hours. Unmold and serve with cottage cheese on crisp salad greens with dill, if desired. Makes about 2 cups or 4 servings.

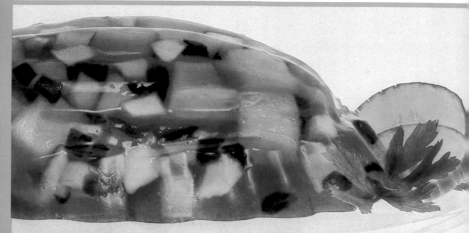

Pineapple-Cucumber Salad

1 can (8-1/4 oz.) chunk pineapple in syrup
1 package (3 oz.) Jell-O brand gelatin, lime flavor
Dash of salt
1 cup boiling water
1 to 2 tablespoons vinegar
1 cup diced cucumber
2 tablespoons finely chopped pimiento

Drain pineapple, reserving syrup. Add water to syrup to make 3/4 cup. Dissolve gelatin and salt in boiling water. Add measured liquid and vinegar and chill until slightly thickened. Fold in pineapple, cucumber and pimiento. Pour into 4-cup mold. Chill until firm. Unmold and garnish with cucumber slices, if desired. Makes 6 servings.

Apple-Cabbage Salad

1 package (3 oz.) Jell-O brand gelatin, lemon flavor
1/2 teaspoon salt
1 cup boiling water
3/4 cup cold water
1 tablespoon vinegar
1 cup diced unpeeled apple
1 cup finely shredded cabbage

Dissolve gelatin and salt in boiling water. Add cold water and vinegar. Chill until thickened. Fold in apple and cabbage. Pour into 3-cup mold. Chill until firm, about 3 hours. Unmold. Makes 3 cups or 6 servings.

Orange-Onion Salad

1 package (3 oz.) Jell-O brand gelatin, lemon, orange or orange-pineapple flavor

1 cup boiling water

2/3 cup cold water

2 teaspoons vinegar

1/8 teaspoon coarsely ground black pepper (optional)

Sections from 3 oranges, drained (about 1-1/2 cups)

1/2 cup thin red onion rings

1/4 cup chopped celery

Dissolve gelatin in boiling water. Add cold water, vinegar and pepper and chill until thickened. Add remaining ingredients. Spoon into 4-cup mold. Chill until firm, at least 4 hours. Unmold. Makes 3-1/2 cups or 7 servings.

Pear-Celery Salad

1 package (3 oz.) Jell-O brand gelatin, cherry or black cherry flavor

Dash of salt

1 cup boiling water

3/4 cup cold water

1/2 cup diced peeled pear

1 small banana, sliced or diced

1/4 cup sliced celery

Dissolve gelatin and salt in boiling water. Add cold water and chill until slightly thickened. Fold in fruits and celery. Spoon into 3-cup mold or individual molds. Chill until firm, about 4 hours. Unmold. Makes 2-1/2 cups or 5 servings.

Two-Way Salad-Dessert

1 package (3 oz.) Jell-O brand gelatin, orange flavor
1 cup boiling water
1/2 cup plain yogurt
1/2 cup shredded carrot
2 tablespoons finely chopped green pepper
1/2 cup drained canned apricot halves
1/2 cup vanilla ice cream

Dissolve gelatin in boiling water. Measure 1/2 cup and chill until slightly thickened. Blend in yogurt. Fold in carrot and green pepper and pour into 2 individual molds. Chill until firm. Unmold and garnish with scallion and carrot curls, if desired. Meanwhile, place apricot halves in 2 individual dessert dishes. Blend ice cream into remaining gelatin. Pour over apricots and chill until set. Garnish with whipped topping and additional fruit, if desired. Makes 2 salads and 2 desserts.

The Family Salad Selector

Want to know what salad to serve with your family meal? Start with the entree, then choose from these suggestions.

With fried chicken...

• Creamy Fruit Salad (Lemon-Peach variation)	54	• Fruit Cocktail Salad	66	
• Melon Salad	63	• Spiced Peaches	66	

With roast chicken, turkey...

• Self-Layering Salad	57	• Florida Sunshine Salad	62
• Cranberry-Sour Cream Mold	60	• Cranberry-Orange Salad	66

With ham...

• Speedy Sunset Salad	57	• Fruit Cocktail Salad	66
• Broccoli-Yogurt Salad	58	• Spiced Peaches	66
• Pineapple-Cottage Cheese	60	• Frozen Fruit Salad	67
• Fruit and Cream Cheese	61	• Pineapple-Cucumber Salad	70

With pork roast or chops...

• Quick Waldorf Salad	56	• Spiced Peaches	66
• Self-Layering Salad	57	• Molded Beet Salad	68
• Strawberry-Banana Squares	63	• Apple-Cabbage Salad	70

With lamb roast or chops...

• Mixed Vegetable Salad	58	• Zucchini Salad	65
• French Bean Basket	59	• Pear-Celery Salad	71

With steak or roast beef...

• Spinach-Cottage Cheese	58	• Tomato Aspic	68
• French Bean Basket	59	• Zesty Spring Salad	68
• Garden Salad	64		

With hamburger, meat loaf...

• Zucchini Salad	65	• Barbecue Cottage Cheese	69
• Tomato Aspic	68	• Two-Way Salad-Dessert	72

With corned beef...

• Molded Beet Salad	68

With frankfurters, cold cuts...

• Pineapple-Cottage Cheese	60	• Barbecue Cottage Cheese	69
• Garden Salad	64		

With seafood...

• Creamy Fruit Salad (Lime-Pineapple variation)	54	• Tomato Aspic	68
		• Pineapple-Cucumber Salad	70
• Yogurt Garden Salad	60	• Orange-Onion Salad	71
• Cucumber-Sour Cream	65		

With cheese or egg entrees...

• Mixed Vegetable Salad	58

With pasta...

• Garden Salad	64	• Zucchini Salad	65

Special Occasion...

These special gelatin salads are destined for stardom—at party buffets, summer picnic tables or any festive meal. The Special Occasion Salad Selector, page 87, will help you choose the one to serve.

Layered Fruit Salad

1 package (3 oz.) Jell-O brand gelatin, lemon flavor

2 cups boiling water

2/3 cup sour cream

1/3 cup mayonnaise

1 tablespoon sugar

2 teaspoons lemon juice

1-1/2 cups coarsely chopped peeled apples

1/4 cup chopped pecans

1 package (3 oz.) Jell-O brand gelatin, cherry flavor

3/4 cup cold water

1 cup halved seedless or pitted green grapes

Dissolve lemon gelatin in 1 cup boiling water; cool slightly. Combine sour cream, mayonnaise, sugar and lemon juice; stir in apples and pecans. Blend sour cream mixture into lemon gelatin. Chill until slightly thickened, about 1 hour.

Dissolve cherry gelatin in 1 cup boiling water. Add cold water. Pour 2/3 cup into 5-cup mold. Chill until set but not firm, about 30 minutes. Arrange 8 to 10 of the grape halves on gelatin and press down gently. Chill remaining cherry gelatin until slightly thickened; add remaining grapes. Spoon lemon gelatin mixture over cherry gelatin in mold and top with remaining cherry gelatin. Chill until firm, about 4 hours. Unmold and garnish with grapes, if desired. Makes 10 servings.

Under-the-Sea Salad

| 1 can (16 oz.) pear halves |
| 1 package (3 oz.) Jell-O brand gelatin, lime flavor |
| 1/4 teaspoon salt (optional) |
| 1 cup boiling water |
| 1 tablespoon lemon juice |
| 2 packages (3 oz. each) cream cheese |
| 1/8 teaspoon cinnamon (optional) |

Drain pears, reserving 3/4 cup of the syrup. Dice pears and set aside.
Dissolve gelatin and salt in boiling water. Add reserved syrup and
lemon juice. Pour 1-1/4 cups into an 8x4-inch loaf pan. Chill until
set but not firm, about 1 hour. Meanwhile, soften cheese until creamy.
Blend in remaining gelatin very slowly, beating until smooth. Add cinnamon and pears and spoon into pan. Chill until firm, about 4 hours.
Unmold and garnish with pear slices and maraschino cherries, if desired. Makes about 3-1/2 cups or 6 servings.
Note: Recipe may be doubled; use a 9x5-inch loaf pan.

Versatile Soufflé Salad

1 package (3 oz.) Jell-O brand gelatin, lemon or lime flavor	
1/4 teaspoon salt	
1 cup boiling water	
1/2 cup cold water	
1/4 cup mayonnaise	
1 to 2-1/2 cups chopped fruits or vegetables	

Dissolve gelatin and salt in boiling water. Add cold water and mayonnaise. Beat until well blended. Pour into 8-inch square pan. Freeze 15 to 20 minutes or until firm about 1 inch from edge but soft in center. Spoon into a bowl and whip until fluffy. Fold in fruits or vegetables. Pour into 8x4-inch loaf pan. Chill in refrigerator (not in freezing unit) until firm, about 30 to 60 minutes. Unmold and garnish with crisp salad greens, if desired. Makes about 4 cups or 8 servings.

Suggested ingredients:
- Raw carrots, cabbage, celery, cucumber, green pepper, radishes, squash, tomatoes or watercress; add 1 to 2 tablespoons vinegar or lemon juice, 1 tablespoon grated onion and dash of pepper with the mayonnaise.
- Cooked asparagus, beets, broccoli, corn, green beans, lima beans, peas or squash; add seasonings as above.
- Fresh or canned fruits, alone or in combinations.

Chinese Salad

  1 package (3 oz.) Jell-O brand gelatin, lemon flavor

  1 cup boiling water

  3/4 cup cold water

1-1/2 tablespoons soy sauce

  1 tablespoon finely chopped scallions*

  1/2 cup grated carrot*

  1/2 cup thinly sliced celery*

  1/2 cup fresh or drained canned bean sprouts*

  1/4 cup thinly sliced water chestnuts (optional)*

*Or use 1 can (16 oz.) mixed Chinese vegetables, drained and rinsed.

Dissolve gelatin in boiling water. Add cold water, soy sauce and scallions and chill until thickened. Fold in vegetables. Pour into 3-cup mold or individual molds. Chill until firm, about 4 hours. Unmold and serve with crisp salad greens, if desired. Makes 3 cups or 6 servings.

Antipasto Salad

  1 package (3 oz.) Jell-O brand gelatin, lemon flavor

1/2 teaspoon salt

  1 cup boiling water

  1 tablespoon vinegar

  2 cups ice cubes

1/2 cup finely cut salami

1/3 cup finely cut Swiss cheese

1/4 cup chopped celery

1/4 cup chopped onion

  2 tablespoons sliced ripe olives

Dissolve gelatin and salt in boiling water. Add vinegar and ice cubes; stir constantly until gelatin begins to thicken, about 3 to 5 minutes. Remove any unmelted ice. Stir in remaining ingredients. Pour into 3-cup serving bowl and chill until firm, about 3 hours. Garnish with ripe olives, if desired. Makes about 2-1/2 cups or 5 servings.

Gazpacho Salad

1 can (7 oz.) pimientos, drained and diced

1-1/2 cups diced unpeeled cucumber

3/4 cup diced green pepper

2 medium tomatoes, diced

4 scallions, sliced

1 cup sliced pitted ripe olives

1 small clove garlic, crushed

2 tablespoons salad oil

1/3 cup vinegar

1 tablespoon salt

1/4 teaspoon pepper

1 can (10-1/2 oz.) consommé

2 packages (3 oz. each) Jell-O brand gelatin, lemon flavor

1-1/2 cups boiling water

Combine pimientos, vegetables, olives, garlic, oil, vinegar, salt and pepper in large bowl. Mix well and stir in consommé. Dissolve gelatin in boiling water. Chill until thickened. Fold in vegetable mixture. Pour into 8-cup mold. Chill until firm, about 4 hours. Unmold and garnish with tomato, lemon and cucumber slices, if desired. Makes 14 servings.

Molded Potato Salad

2 to 3 tablespoons vinegar

1 envelope Good Seasons mild Italian salad dressing mix

3 cups diced cold cooked potatoes

2 strips crisp bacon, finely crumbled

1 package (3 oz.) Jell-O brand gelatin, lemon flavor

1 cup boiling water

1/4 cup cold water

1-1/2 cups mayonnaise

Combine vinegar and salad dressing mix. Add to potatoes and bacon and chill about 1 hour. Dissolve gelatin in boiling water; add cold water. Blend in mayonnaise and chill until thickened. Add potato mixture and pour into 6-cup mold or metal bowl. Chill until firm, about 4 hours. Unmold and garnish with scallion leaves and vegetable flowers, if desired. Makes about 5 cups or 10 servings.

Macaroni Salad

1 cup cooked elbow macaroni
1/2 cup diced celery
2 tablespoons chopped dill pickle
2 tablespoons chopped pimiento
1/4 cup mayonnaise
1 teaspoon salt
1/2 teaspoon grated onion
1/2 teaspoon Worcestershire sauce
1 package (3 oz.) Jell-O brand gelatin, lemon flavor
1 cup boiling water
3/4 cup cold water

Combine macaroni, celery, pickle, pimiento, mayonnaise, salt, onion and Worcestershire sauce in a bowl. Mix well and chill. Dissolve gelatin in boiling water. Add cold water and chill until slightly thickened. Fold in macaroni mixture. Spoon into individual molds. Chill until firm, about 3 hours. Unmold. Makes 3 cups or 6 servings.

Old-Fashioned Coleslaw Mold

1 package (3 oz.) Jell-O brand gelatin, lemon flavor
1/2 teaspoon salt
1 cup boiling water
1/2 cup cold water
2 tablespoons vinegar
1/2 cup mayonnaise
1/2 cup sour cream
1 tablespoon prepared mustard
1 teaspoon grated onion
3 cups shredded cabbage
2 tablespoons diced pimiento
1 tablespoon chopped parsley

Dissolve gelatin and salt in boiling water. Add cold water and vinegar. Stir in mayonnaise, sour cream, mustard and onion, blending thoroughly. Chill until thickened. Fold in cabbage, pimiento and parsley. Pour into 4-cup mold or serving bowl. Chill until firm, about 3 hours. Unmold. Makes 4 cups or 8 servings.

Party Cranberry Salad

> 3 packages (3 oz. each) Jell-O brand gelatin, raspberry flavor

> 4 cups boiling water

> 1 cup cold water

3/4 cup port wine

> 1 cup whole berry cranberry sauce

1/2 cup chopped apple

1/2 cup chopped walnuts

> 1 package (3 oz.) Jell-O brand gelatin, lemon flavor

1/2 cup mayonnaise

> 1 container (4 oz.) Cool Whip non-dairy whipped topping, thawed

Dissolve 1 package raspberry gelatin in 1 cup of the boiling water. Add 1/4 cup of the cold water and 1/4 cup of the wine and chill until slightly thickened. Fold in cranberry sauce, apple and walnuts. Pour into 2-1/2-quart serving bowl or mold. Chill until set but not firm. Dissolve lemon gelatin in 1 cup of the boiling water. Chill until slightly thickened, then blend in mayonnaise and whipped topping. Pour over gelatin in bowl. Chill until set but not firm. Dissolve remaining raspberry gelatin in remaining 2 cups boiling water. Add remaining 3/4 cup cold water and 1/2 cup wine. Chill until slightly thickened. Pour into bowl over lemon layer. Chill until firm. Garnish with green grapes and cranberries, if desired. Makes 10 cups or 20 servings.

Party Avocado Ring

> 4 packages (3 oz. each) or 2 packages (6 oz. each) Jell-O brand gelatin, lemon or lime flavor

1-1/2 teaspoons salt

> 4 cups boiling water

> 3 cups cold water

1/4 cup lemon juice

> 4 fully ripe avocados, peeled, pitted and mashed

3/4 cup mayonnaise

Dissolve gelatin and salt in boiling water. Add cold water and chill until thickened. Stir lemon juice into avocados and add to gelatin with the mayonnaise, blending well. Pour into 12-cup ring mold or two 6-cup ring molds. Chill until firm, at least 6 hours or overnight. Unmold. Makes about 10 cups or 20 servings.

Muffin-Pan Buffet Salad

2 packages (3 oz. each) or 1 package (6 oz.) Jell-O brand
gelatin, lemon flavor

1/2 teaspoon salt

1/2 teaspoon garlic salt

3 cups boiling water

1 tablespoon vinegar

2 teaspoons salad oil

4 dashes black pepper

4 dashes oregano

Salad ingredients*

Dissolve gelatin, salt and garlic salt in boiling water. Add vinegar, oil,
pepper and oregano. Put foil cupcake liners into muffin pans. Place
one of the suggested salad ingredients in each liner, filling each about
2/3 full. Then fill with gelatin mixture. Chill until firm, about 2 hours.
Unmold carefully from foil cups. Serve with crisp salad greens, if
desired. Makes 8 cups or 16 to 20 servings.

*Suggested ingredients:
- Flaked drained tuna with capers and chopped chives
- Cauliflower florets and diced pimiento
- Sliced celery with chopped pickles or olives
- Cucumber and tomato slices
- Sliced hard-cooked egg with anchovy
- Drained canned button mushrooms with
  pimiento strips
- Sliced pickles with shredded cabbage
- Cooked cut green beans with cubed
  cream cheese

Vegetable Trio

2 packages (3 oz. each) Jell-O brand gelatin, lemon flavor	
1 teaspoon salt	
2 cups boiling water	
1-1/2 cups cold water	
3 tablespoons vinegar	
1-1/2 cups shredded carrots	
1/2 cup mayonnaise	
1 cup finely chopped cabbage	
1-1/2 cups finely chopped spinach	
1 teaspoon grated onion	

Dissolve gelatin and salt in boiling water. Add cold water and vinegar. Measure 1-1/3 cups into a bowl. Place bowl in larger bowl of ice and water and stir until slightly thickened. Stir in carrots and pour into 6-cup mold or 9x5-inch loaf pan. Chill until set but not firm. Measure 1 cup of remaining gelatin and blend in mayonnaise. Chill over ice until thickened. Stir in cabbage and spoon into mold; chill. Chill remaining gelatin over ice until slightly thickened. Add spinach and onion and spoon into mold. Chill until firm, about 3 hours. Unmold and garnish with carrot curls, if desired. Makes 5-1/2 cups or 10 servings.

Melon-Nut Layered Salad

2 packages (3 oz. each) or 1 package (6 oz.) Jell-O brand gelatin, orange, lime or lemon flavor

Dash of salt

2 cups boiling water

1-1/2 cups cold water

2 teaspoons lemon juice

1 to 2 cups small melon balls

1/2 cup sliced celery

1/2 cup finely slivered almonds (optional)

2 packages (3 oz. each) cream cheese, softened

4 tablespoons mayonnaise

Dissolve gelatin and salt in boiling water. Add cold water and lemon juice. Chill until slightly thickened. Fold melon balls, celery and almonds into 1-1/4 cups of the gelatin. Pour into 6-cup mold. Chill until set but not firm. Combine cream cheese and mayonnaise, blending until smooth. Gradually blend in remaining gelatin. Pour over gelatin in mold. Chill until firm, about 4 hours. Unmold and serve with crisp salad greens and additional melon balls, if desired. Makes about 6 cups or 12 servings.

Ribbon Salad

1 package (3 oz.) Jell-O brand gelatin, lemon flavor

1 package (3 oz.) Jell-O brand gelatin, cherry, raspberry or strawberry flavor

1 package (3 oz.) Jell-O brand gelatin, lime flavor

3 cups boiling water

1 package (8 oz.) cream cheese, softened

1 can (8-1/4 oz.) crushed pineapple in syrup

1 cup thawed Cool Whip non-dairy whipped topping

1/2 cup mayonnaise

1-1/2 cups cold water

Dissolve each flavor of gelatin separately in 1 cup of the boiling water. Gradually blend lemon gelatin mixture into softened cream cheese, beating until smooth. Add pineapple with syrup and chill until slightly thickened. Blend in whipped topping and mayonnaise and chill until very thick.

Meanwhile, add 3/4 cup cold water to the cherry gelatin; pour into 9-inch square pan and chill until set but not firm. Add remaining cold water to the lime gelatin; chill until slightly thickened. Spoon lemon gelatin mixture over the cherry gelatin layer. Chill until set but not firm; top with lime gelatin. Chill until firm, at least 4 hours or overnight. Unmold and garnish with cut-up canned pineapple slices and maraschino cherries, if desired. Makes 8 cups or 16 servings.

The Special Occasion Salad Selector

When you're entertaining, what gelatin salad will you serve with your special entree? Try these suggestions.

With roast chicken or turkey...

• Party Cranberry Salad	82		

With other chicken dishes...

• Versatile Soufflé Salad	77	• Melon-Nut Layered Salad	85

With duck, Cornish game hen...

• Layered Fruit Salad	74		

With ham...

• Versatile Soufflé Salad	77	• Ribbon Salad	86

With pork...

• Layered Fruit Salad	74	• Versatile Soufflé Salad	77

With lamb...

• Under-the-Sea Salad	76		

With steak, roast beef...

• Gazpacho Salad	79		

With frankfurters, hamburgers...

• Molded Potato Salad	80	• Macaroni Salad	81

With barbecued meats...

• Gazpacho Salad	79	• Vegetable Trio	84

With seafood...

• Gazpacho Salad	79	• Party Avocado Ring	82
• Old-Fashioned Coleslaw Mold	81	• Vegetable Trio	84

With pasta, Italian dishes...

• Antipasto Salad	78		

With Mexican or Spanish dishes...

• Gazpacho Salad	79	• Party Avocado Ring	82

With Chinese dishes...

• Chinese Salad	78		

With curry dishes...

• Party Avocado Ring	82		

With a mixed buffet...

• Muffin-Pan Buffet Salad (with many variations)	83		

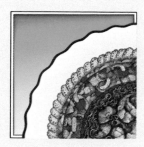

Introducing a delightful plan for cool summer dining, a special light luncheon—the entree salad. It's flavorful and decorative, with a refreshing mix of ingredients, piquant and mild.

Shimmering Shrimp Mold

2 packages (3 oz. each) or 1 package (6 oz.) Jell-O brand gelatin, lemon or lime flavor

2 teaspoons salt

2 cups boiling water

1 cup cold water

4 teaspoons vinegar

2 cups small cooked shrimp*

1/2 cup diced celery

2 tablespoons chopped pimiento

1 cup (1/2 pt.) sour cream or yogurt

1 tablespoon chopped parsley

1 tablespoon chopped onion

1 teaspoon curry powder (optional)

*Or use diced cooked ham or turkey.

Dissolve gelatin and salt in boiling water. Add cold water and vinegar and chill until thickened. Add 1-1/2 cups of the shrimp, the celery and pimiento to 1-1/2 cups of the gelatin and spoon into 6-cup ring mold. Chill until set but not firm. Add sour cream, parsley, onion and curry to remaining gelatin; spoon into mold. Chill until firm, about 4 hours. Unmold and serve with salad greens, if desired. Garnish with remaining shrimp. Makes about 6 cups or 6 to 8 entree servings.

Nicoise Salad Mold

1 can (7 oz.) tuna, drained and coarsely flaked

1 small tomato, diced and drained

1/2 cup cooked cut green beans (optional)

2 tablespoons sliced ripe olives

2 tablespoons green pepper strips

2 tablespoons red onion strips

2 tablespoons prepared French or Italian salad dressing

1 package (3 oz.) Jell-O brand gelatin, lemon flavor

1/2 teaspoon salt

1 cup boiling water

1/2 cup cold water

2 teaspoons vinegar

1 hard-cooked egg, diced

2 cups coarsely chopped lettuce

1/2 cup mayonnaise

2 tablespoons cream or milk

2 anchovy fillets, finely chopped (optional)

Combine tuna, vegetables and French dressing in bowl. Mix lightly; let stand to marinate. Dissolve gelatin and salt in boiling water. Add cold water and vinegar and chill until slightly thickened. Spoon vegetable mixture and diced egg into 6-cup ring mold. Pour on half the gelatin mixture; spread lettuce on top. Add remaining gelatin and chill until firm, about 4 hours. Unmold and serve with mixture of mayonnaise, cream and anchovies. Garnish with watercress, if desired. Makes about 5 cups or 6 entree servings.

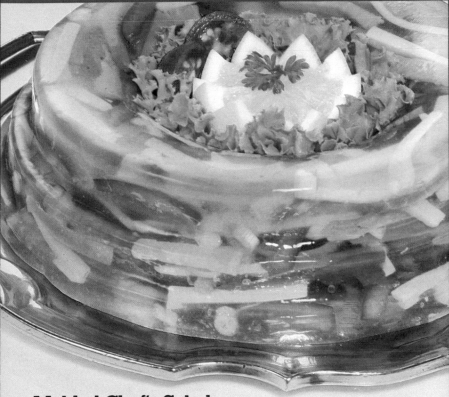

Molded Chef's Salad

2 packages (3 oz. each) or 1 package (6 oz.) Jell-O brand
  gelatin, lemon or lime flavor

2 teaspoons salt

2 cups boiling water

1 cup cold water

3 tablespoons vinegar

3/4 cup thin cooked ham strips (about 4 oz.)

3/4 cup thin Swiss or process American cheese strips
  (about 4 oz.)

1/4 cup finely sliced scallions or red onion

1/2 small green pepper, cut in strips

Dissolve gelatin and salt in boiling water. Add cold water and vinegar
and chill until thickened. Fold in remaining ingredients. Pour into
5-cup mold or metal mixing bowl. Chill until firm, at least 6 hours or
overnight. Unmold and garnish with lemon and tomato wedges, if
desired. Makes 4-1/2 cups or 4 entree servings.

Molded Crab Louis

2 packages (3 oz. each) or 1 package (6 oz.) Jell-O brand gelatin, lemon flavor

1/2 teaspoon salt

2 cups boiling water

1/2 cup sour cream

1/2 cup mayonnaise

1/4 cup chili sauce

2 tablespoons grated onion

2 tablespoons lemon juice

2 tablespoons dry sherry wine

2 cans (6 oz. each) crab meat, drained and flaked

1/2 cup chopped celery

1/4 cup chopped pimiento

Dissolve gelatin and salt in boiling water. Blend in sour cream, mayonnaise, chili sauce, onion, lemon juice and wine and chill until thickened. Fold in crab, celery and pimiento. Spoon into 6-cup mold. Chill until firm, about 4 hours. Unmold. Makes 5-1/2 cups or 5 entree servings.

Creamy Fish Salad

2 packages (3 oz. each) or 1 package (6 oz.) Jell-O brand gelatin, lemon flavor

2 teaspoons salt

2 cups boiling water

1 cup cold water

1 tablespoon vinegar

1 cup (1/2 pt.) sour cream

1 package (16 oz.) frozen fish fillets, cooked and flaked

1/2 cup diced celery

2 tablespoons chopped pimiento

1 tablespoon chopped parsley

1 tablespoon chopped onion

1 teaspoon curry powder (optional)

Dissolve gelatin and salt in boiling water. Add cold water and vinegar and chill until slightly thickened. Add sour cream, blending until smooth.

Stir in remaining ingredients and spoon into 6-cup mold. Chill until firm, about 4 hours. Unmold and serve with crisp salad greens, if desired. Makes about 6 cups or 6 entree servings.

Salmon Dill Mousse

2 packages (3 oz. each) or 1 package (6 oz.) Jell-O brand gelatin, lemon flavor

2 cups boiling water

1 cup cold water

3 tablespoons lemon juice or vinegar

1 can (15 or 16 oz.) red or pink salmon, drained and flaked

1/2 cup sour cream

1/4 cup mayonnaise

2 tablespoons minced onion

1-1/2 teaspoons dill weed

Dissolve gelatin in boiling water. Add cold water and lemon juice and chill until thickened. Mix salmon with sour cream, mayonnaise, onion and dill and blend into gelatin. Pour into 6-cup fish mold or 8x4-inch loaf pan. Chill until firm, about 4 hours. Unmold and garnish with stuffed olive "eye," cucumber and lemon slices and dill, if desired. Makes 5-1/3 cups or 5 or 6 entree servings.

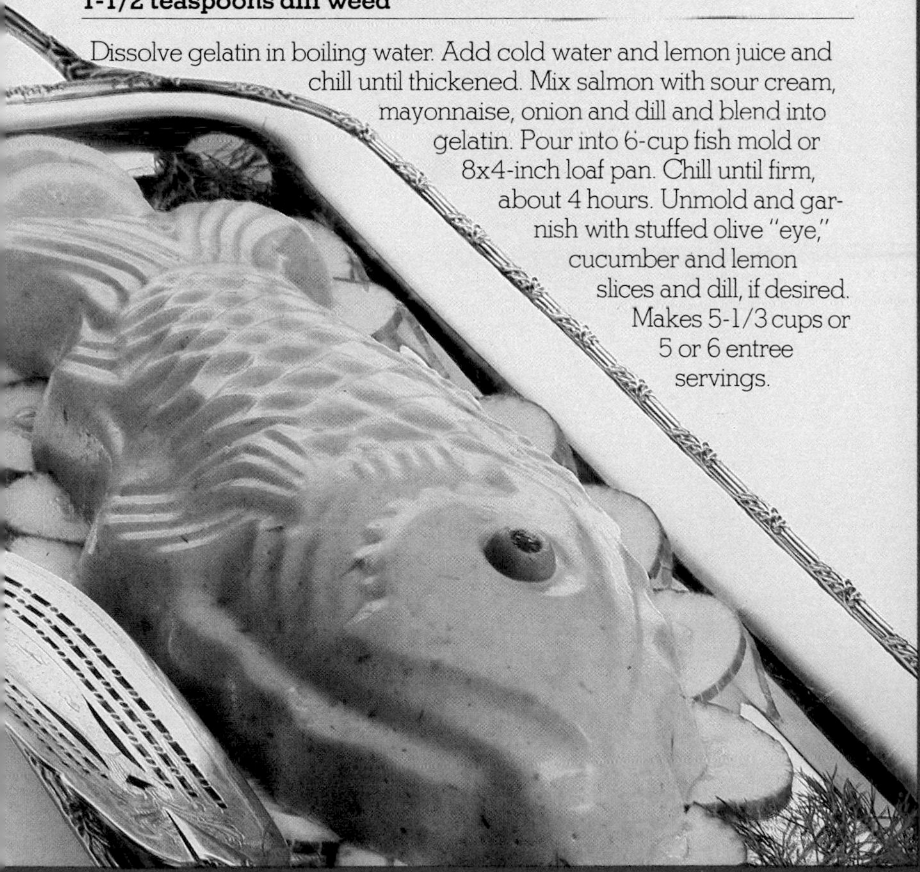

Salmagundi Salad

2 packages (3 oz. each) or 1 package (6 oz.) Jell-O brand
gelatin, lemon flavor

1/2 teaspoon salt

2 cups boiling water

1-1/2 cups cold water

1 tablespoon vinegar

1/4 cup pimiento strips

1/4 cup halved pitted ripe olives

2 cups finely diced cooked ham or chicken

2 hard-cooked eggs, chopped

1/4 cup chopped green pepper

1/4 cup sweet pickle relish

2 tablespoons grated onion

1 tablespoon prepared horseradish

1/2 cup mayonnaise

1/2 cup sour cream

1 teaspoon Worcestershire sauce

1 teaspoon prepared mustard

Dissolve gelatin and salt in boiling water. Add cold water and vinegar.
Measure 1/2 cup, pour into 6-cup ring mold and chill until set but not
firm. Arrange pimiento and olives on set gelatin and add another 1/2
cup gelatin. Chill until set but not firm.

Chill remaining gelatin until thickened. Add ham, eggs, green pepper, relish, onion and horseradish. Spoon into mold and chill until firm, at least 4 hours.

Combine remaining ingredients and chill. Unmold salad and serve with dressing. Makes 5 cups or 5 entree servings.

Molded Chicken and Grape Salad

1 package (3 oz.) Jell-O brand gelatin, lemon or lime flavor

1/2 teaspoon salt

1 cup boiling water

1/8 teaspoon tarragon

3/4 cup cold water

2 teaspoons lemon juice

1 cup diced cooked chicken or turkey

1/4 pound green or purple grapes, halved and seeded (about 3/4 cup)

1/2 cup diced celery

Dissolve gelatin and salt in boiling water; add tarragon. Add cold water and lemon juice and chill until thickened. Stir in remaining ingredients. Spoon into 4-cup mold or individual molds. Chill until firm, about 4 hours. Unmold and serve with mayonnaise. Makes about 3-1/2 cups or 4 entree servings.

Jellied Ham Loaf

2 packages (3 oz. each) or 1 package (6 oz.) Jell-O brand gelatin, lemon flavor

2 cups boiling water

1 cup catsup

1 cup mayonnaise

1-1/2 cups ground cooked ham (about 6 oz.)

1 cup minced celery

1/2 cup finely chopped green pepper

Dissolve gelatin in boiling water. Stir in catsup. Chill until slightly thickened. Blend in mayonnaise, then add ham, celery and green pepper. Pour into 8x4-inch loaf pan. Chill until firm, about 4 hours. Unmold and serve with additional mayonnaise and hard-cooked egg slices, if desired. Makes 6 cups or 6 entree servings.

Kids' Stuff

Now the small fry get into the act, with snacks they can make them-
selves and desserts to make for the family. They're just following tradi-
tion, for Jell-O gelatin has long been a favorite with young cooks.

Jellied Joker

1 jar (17 oz.) fruits for salad

2 packages (3 oz. each) Jell-O brand gelatin, peach flavor

2 cups boiling water

Drain fruits, reserving syrup. Add water to syrup to make 1-1/2 cups.
Dissolve gelatin in boiling water. Add measured liquid. Pour 1 cup
gelatin into an 8-inch layer pan and chill until set but not firm. Arrange
fruits on gelatin to resemble a face; reserve remaining fruit. Pour about
1/2 cup gelatin around fruits; chill a few minutes until set and pour on
remaining gelatin. Chill until firm, about 3 hours. Unmold on serving
plate. Cut in wedges and serve with remaining fruit. Makes about
4-1/2 cups or 8 servings.

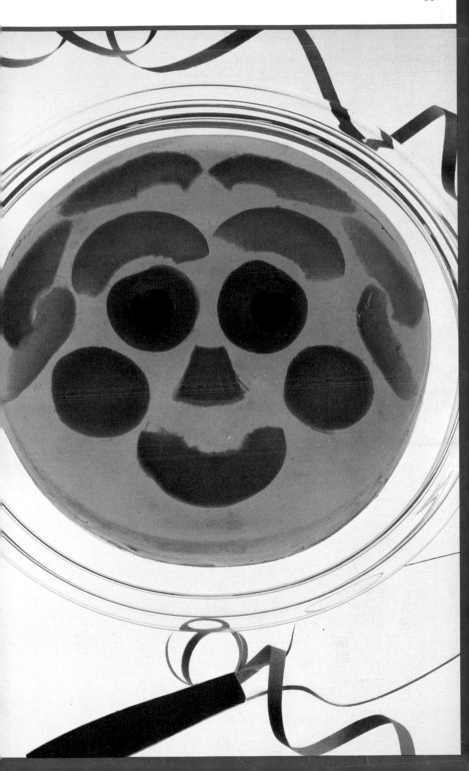

Gelatin-Wiches

1 package (3 oz.) Jell-O brand gelatin, peach flavor

1 cup boiling water

1 container (4 oz.) Cool Whip non-dairy whipped topping, thawed

14 double graham crackers, separated

Dissolve gelatin in boiling water and chill until slightly thickened. Fold in whipped topping. Spread gelatin mixture about 1/2 inch thick on 14 of the crackers; top with remaining crackers, pressing lightly and smoothing around edges with spatula. Freeze until firm, about 3 hours. Makes 14 sandwiches.

Fruit Flavor Frozen Cups

1 package (3 oz.) Jell-O brand gelatin, any flavor

1/2 cup sugar

2 cups boiling water

2 cups cold water

Dissolve gelatin and sugar in boiling water. Add cold water and pour into plastic or paper cups, soufflé cups or pop molds. Freeze until almost firm, about 2 hours. Insert wooden spoons or sticks. Freeze until firm, 8 hours or overnight. Makes 28 small or 8 or 9 large pops.

Gelatin Cones

    1 package (3 oz.) Jell-O brand gelatin, any flavor

    1 cup boiling water

    1 cup cold water

    4 flat-bottom ice cream cones

1/2 cup thawed Cool Whip non-dairy whipped topping

Dissolve gelatin in boiling water. Add cold water and chill in bowl until set. Spoon set gelatin into ice cream cones. Top with dollops of whipped topping and multicolored sprinkles, if desired. Serve at once. Makes 4 servings.

Gelatin Jiggles

    4 packages (3 oz. each) Jell-O brand gelatin, any flavor

2-1/2 cups boiling water

Dissolve gelatin completely in boiling water in a bowl. Pour into 9-inch square pan. Chill until firm, about 4 hours. Cut into 1-inch squares or use cookie cutters to cut into decorative shapes. Makes 81 squares or 16 to 24 shapes.

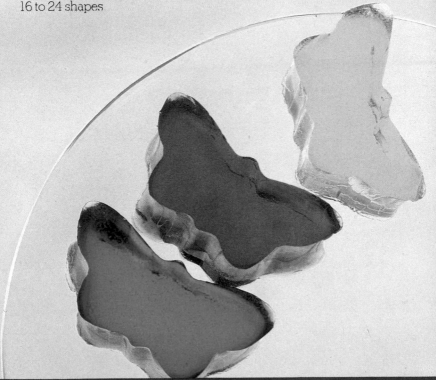

Supersodas

1 package (3 oz.) Jell-O brand gelatin, any flavor

1 cup boiling water

1 cup club soda

1/4 cup cold water

1 cup (1/2 pt.) vanilla ice cream

Thawed Cool Whip non-dairy whipped topping

Dissolve gelatin in boiling water. Add club soda and cold water and chill until slightly thickened. Measure 1 cup into a small bowl and set aside. Place a small scoop of ice cream in each of three 12-ounce soda glasses. Fill glasses two-thirds full with slightly thickened gelatin. Beat reserved gelatin until light and fluffy and spoon into glasses. Chill until firm, about 2 hours. Top with whipped topping and mint leaves, if desired.
Makes 3 servings.

Root Beer Fizz

1 package (3 oz.) Jell-O brand gelatin, any flavor

1 cup boiling root beer or cola beverage

1-1/2 cups crushed ice

8 plastic straws (optional)

Combine gelatin and boiling root beer in electric blender container. Cover and blend at low speed until gelatin is dissolved, about 1 minute. Add crushed ice and blend at high speed until ice is melted, about 30 seconds. Pour into 6-ounce soda glasses and insert straws. Serve at once, or chill until set, about 30 minutes. Makes 4 servings.

Fruity Sundaes

1 package (3 oz.) Jell-O brand gelatin, any flavor
1 cup boiling water
1-1/4 cups cold water
1 pint ice cream, any flavor
1/2 cup fruit sundae sauce or drained fruit
1 cup thawed Cool Whip non-dairy whipped topping
1/4 cup chopped nuts
4 stemmed maraschino cherries

Dissolve gelatin in boiling water. Add cold water and chill in bowl until set. Alternately spoon ice cream and gelatin into 4 tall sundae glasses, ending with gelatin, filling to within 1/2 inch of tops. Top with sauce, whipped topping, nuts and cherries. Serve at once. Makes 4 servings.

Banana Splits

1 package (3 oz.) Jell-O brand gelatin, any flavor
1 cup boiling water
3/4 cup cold water
4 bananas
1 cup thawed Cool Whip whipped topping
1/2 cup chopped nuts

Dissolve gelatin in boiling water. Add cold water and pour into shallow pan. Chill until firm. Break into small flakes with a fork, or force through potato ricer or large-meshed strainer. Split bananas lengthwise and arrange in 4 oblong serving dishes. Top with flaked gelatin. Garnish with whipped topping and sprinkle with nuts. Makes 4 servings.

Pastel Cupcakes

1 package (2-layer size) white cake mix

1 package (3 oz.) Jell-O brand gelatin, any flavor

1/4 cup boiling water

6 tablespoons butter or margarine

3 cups confectioners sugar

Prepare cake mix as directed on package for cupcakes, adding 1/2 package (about 4 tablespoons) of the gelatin before beating. Cool 10 minutes in pans. Remove from pans and finish cooling on racks. Dissolve remaining gelatin in the boiling water. Cream butter; add part of the sugar gradually, blending after each addition. Add remaining sugar alternately with gelatin mixture, beating until smooth. Spread on tops of cupcakes. Decorate with colored sprinkles, gumdrop flowers or candy decorations, if desired. Makes 24 to 30 cupcakes.

In high altitude areas, increase egg whites to 3 and water to 1-1/2 cups; add 2/3 cup all-purpose flour; bake at 375° for 15 to 20 minutes.

Orange Ginger Whip

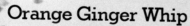

1 bottle (7 fl. oz.) ginger ale

1 package (3 oz.) Jell-O brand gelatin, orange flavor

1 cup cold orange juice

Bring ginger ale to a boil. Add to gelatin and stir until dissolved. Add orange juice. Place bowl of gelatin in larger bowl of ice and water. Stir until slightly thickened, then whip with rotary beater or electric mixer until fluffy and thick and about double in volume. Spoon into individual dessert dishes and chill until set, at least 30 minutes. Makes 4 cups or 6 servings.

Rosy Glazed Apples

1 package (3 oz.) Jell-O brand gelatin, raspberry or strawberry flavor

3/4 cup water

1/8 teaspoon ground cinnamon

2 lemon slices, 1/4 inch thick

4 medium baking apples, peeled and cored

Combine gelatin, water, cinnamon and lemon slices in medium skillet. Cook and stir over medium heat until mixture comes to a boil and gelatin is dissolved. Add apples; cover and simmer 10 to 15 minutes, or until almost tender, turning once and basting occasionally. Remove from heat. Cool apples in syrup. Remove lemon slices. Place apples in individual serving dishes or custard cups. Chill gelatin mixture until slightly thickened. Spoon over apples to glaze. Chill until set, about 1 hour. Serve with whipped topping, if desired. Makes 4 servings.

Marshmallow Parfait

1 package (3 oz.) Jell-O brand gelatin, any flavor

1 cup boiling water

1 cup cold water

Miniature marshmallows

Dissolve gelatin in boiling water. Add cold water. Measure 2/3 cup and chill until slightly thickened. Whip with rotary beater or electric mixer until fluffy and thick; chill until set. Chill remaining gelatin until set. Spoon half the clear gelatin into 4 parfait glasses. Add a layer of marshmallows and spoon in whipped gelatin. Top with remaining clear gelatin and garnish with additional marshmallows, if desired. Makes 4 servings.

Carousels

1 package (3 oz.) Jell-O brand gelatin, any red flavor

1 cup boiling water

1 cup cold water

Animal crackers

Candy sticks

Thawed Cool Whip non-dairy whipped topping

Dissolve gelatin in boiling water. Add cold water and pour into individual serving dishes. Chill until almost firm, then arrange animal crackers around inside rim of glass; insert a candy stick in center of gelatin. Chill until firm. Decorate base of candy stick with whipped topping. Makes 4 servings.

Banana Wobbler

1 package (3 oz.) Jell-O brand gelatin, any flavor

1 cup boiling water

1/2 cup cold water

3 empty 6-ounce cans

2 medium bananas, cut in half

Dissolve gelatin in boiling water. Add cold water and chill until thickened. Place a spoonful of gelatin in each can, center the banana halves and spoon remaining gelatin around bananas. Chill until firm, about 2 hours. Dip remaining banana half in lemon juice and set aside. Dip each can to the rim in warm water; invert onto plate, puncture bottom and lift off can. Cut each mold in slices. Serve with whipped topping, if desired. Garnish with reserved banana, sliced. Makes 3 or 4 servings.

Clown Faces

1 package (3 oz.) Jell-O brand gelatin, any flavor

1 cup boiling water

1 cup cold water

Thawed Cool Whip non-dairy whipped topping

Hard candies with center holes

Dissolve gelatin in boiling water. Add cold water and pour into individual serving dishes. Chill until firm. Garnish with whipped topping and decorate face with candies, using whole candies for eyes, half a candy for mouth and a piece for the nose. Makes 4 servings.

Pinstripe Parfaits

1 package (3 oz.) Jell-O brand gelatin, cherry, strawberry or raspberry flavor

1 cup boiling water

1 cup cold water

Light cream, half and half or milk

Dissolve gelatin in boiling water. Add cold water and pour into parfait glasses, filling to about 1 inch from tops. Chill until firm. Pour cream over top of set gelatin, about 1/2 inch deep. With drinking straw, make deep tunnels at intervals around ouside of gelatin, allowing cream to settle into the tunnels. Makes 4 servings.

Ready for some new ideas? Here are marvelous new ways with gelatin —from appetizers and soups to go-withs for your entrees, as well as extra-special confections. And Jell-O gelatin makes them happen.

Marzipan

1 package (3 oz.) Jell-O brand gelatin, any flavor
1 cup ground blanched almonds
1-3/4 cups (about) Baker's cookie coconut
2/3 cup sweetened condensed milk
1-1/2 teaspoons sugar
1 teaspoon almond extract
Food coloring (optional)

Thoroughly mix all ingredients. Shape into small fruits or vegetables by hand or with small candy molds. If desired, use food coloring to paint details on fruit; add whole cloves and citron or angelica for stems and blossom ends. Chill until dry, then store at room temperature in covered container. Makes about 24 to 36 confections.

Appropriate flavors:
- Strawberry flavor gelatin for strawberries
- Lemon flavor gelatin for grapefruit, bananas, lemons, pears
- Lime flavor gelatin for green apples, green pears, limes
- Orange flavor gelatin for carrots, pumpkins, tangerines, oranges
- Cherry flavor gelatin for cherries

Jellied Cucumber Soup

1 can (12 oz.) chicken broth

1 cup water

2 tablespoons chopped onion

2 tablespoons chopped green pepper

2 tablespoons chopped parsley

2 whole cloves

1 package (3 oz.) Jell-O brand gelatin, lime flavor

3 tablespoons vinegar

1 teaspoon salt

1/4 teaspoon dill weed

Dash of pepper

1 cup milk

1 cup (1/2 pt.) sour cream

1 cup chopped or grated cucumber

Combine broth, water, onion, green pepper, parsley and cloves in saucepan. Bring to a boil; cover and simmer 10 minutes. Strain, discarding vegetables and cloves. Dissolve gelatin in the hot liquid. Stir in vinegar, salt, dill weed and pepper. Chill until slightly thickened.

Combine milk and sour cream, blending until smooth. Fold into gelatin mixture with cucumber. Chill in bowl until set, about 3 hours. Stir gently before serving and spoon into chilled soup cups. Garnish with chopped chives, if desired. Makes 5-1/3 cups or 6 to 8 servings.

Egg Slices in Aspic

1 can (10-1/2 oz.) condensed beef broth

1 package (3 oz.) Jell-O brand gelatin, lemon flavor

1/2 cup Madeira wine

1/8 teaspoon hot pepper sauce

1 tablespoon chopped pimiento

8 hard-cooked egg slices (2 eggs)

8 toasted bread rounds or sesame seed crackers

Bring broth to a boil. Add to gelatin and stir until dissolved. Add wine and pepper sauce. Measure about 3 tablespoons of the gelatin, add pimiento and spoon evenly into 8 relish molds or small tart pans. Chill until set but not firm. Place an egg slice in each mold and add remaining gelatin. Chill until firm, about 2 hours. Unmold onto toast rounds. Makes 8 appetizer servings.

Continental Cheese Mold

1 package (3 oz.) Jell-O brand gelatin, lemon flavor
3/4 cup boiling water
1 container (16 oz.) cottage cheese (2 cups)
1/2 cup sour cream
1/4 pound Roquefort or bleu cheese, softened
2 teaspoons seasoned salt
3/4 teaspoon Worcestershire sauce
1/2 teaspoon lemon juice
2 tablespoons finely cut chives or parsley

Dissolve gelatin in boiling water. Combine cottage cheese, sour cream, Roquefort cheese, salt, Worcestershire sauce and lemon juice in a large bowl and beat with rotary beater until smooth. Or combine ingredients in electric blender container and blend until smooth. Gradually blend in gelatin mixture. Add chives and pour into 4-cup mold. Chill until firm, about 3 hours. Unmold and serve as appetizer with assorted crackers and fresh vegetables. Makes 4 cups.

Molded Tomato Relish

1 can (16 oz.) stewed tomatoes

1 package (3 oz.) Jell-O brand gelatin, lemon or strawberry flavor

1/2 teaspoon salt

1 tablespoon vinegar

Pour tomatoes into saucepan, saving can to use as a mold. Bring tomatoes to a boil; reduce heat and simmer 2 minutes. Add gelatin, salt and vinegar and stir until gelatin is dissolved. Pour into can and chill until firm, about 4 hours. To unmold, dip can in warm water and puncture bottom. Makes about 2 cups or 6 servings.

Minted Glazed Pears

3 medium pears, peeled, halved and cored

1 cup water

1/3 cup sugar

1 package (3 oz.) Jell-O brand gelatin, lime flavor

1/2 teaspoon mint extract

Place pears in saucepan with water and sugar. Bring to a boil and boil gently 10 minutes. Remove from heat. Add gelatin and stir until dissolved. Add mint extract. Continue boiling, basting frequently until pears are glazed, about 20 minutes. Serve as meat accompaniment. Makes 6 servings.

Pineapple-Mint Relish

1 package (3 oz.) Jell-O brand gelatin, lime flavor

Dash of salt

3/4 cup boiling water

1 can (15-1/4 oz.) crushed pineapple in syrup

4 drops mint or peppermint extract

1 tablespoon vinegar

Dissolve gelatin and salt in boiling water. Stir in remaining ingredients and chill until thickened. Pour into 3- or 4-cup mold, individual molds or a serving bowl. Chill until firm, about 4 hours. Unmold. Makes about 2-1/2 cups or 7 relish servings.

Jellied Chutney Relish

6 whole cloves

1-3/4 cups water

1 package (3 oz.) Jell-O brand gelatin, apricot or lemon flavor

1/2 teaspoon salt

1/2 cup chutney, drained and finely chopped

1 teaspoon prepared horseradish

Bring cloves and 1 cup of the water to a boil in saucepan; boil 3 minutes. Remove and discard cloves. Dissolve gelatin and salt in hot liquid. Add remaining water and chill until thickened. Add chutney and horseradish. Pour into bowl or 9x5-inch loaf pan. Chill until firm, about 3 hours. Spoon into relish dish or cut in squares. Makes about 2 cups or 6 relish servings.

Pastel Candied Fruit Peel

3 large grapefruit or 6 large oranges (free from blemishes)
2 packages (3 oz. each) or 1 package (6 oz.) Jell-O brand gelatin, any flavor
2 cups water
1 cup sugar
1 large stick cinnamon
1/2 teaspoon whole cloves
1 cup (about) sugar

Cut fruit in halves. Squeeze juice; strain and use as desired. Cover rinds with water in saucepan. Bring to a boil and boil 15 minutes. Drain. Carefully remove any remaining pulp and all the white membrane, using bowl of spoon. Cut peel with scissors or sharp knife into thin strips about 1/4 inch wide. Place in saucepan with water to cover. Boil again for 15 minutes, or until easily pierced with a fork. Drain.

Mix gelatin with 2 cups water and 1 cup sugar in heavy skillet. Add prepared fruit peels and spices. Bring to a boil; reduce heat and continue cooking, stirring occasionally until peels are translucent and syrup is almost all absorbed, 35 to 40 minutes. Remove from heat. Lift peels from skillet with fork or slotted spoon. Sprinkle with 1 cup sugar and toss lightly. Arrange pieces in a single layer on waxed paper-lined trays; let dry about 12 hours or overnight. Store in tightly covered container. Makes about 1 pound.

Fig-Berry Preserves

3 cups finely chopped figs (about 20 medium figs)
2 packages (3 oz. each) or 1 package (6 oz.) Jell-O brand gelatin, strawberry flavor
3 cups (1-1/4 lb.) sugar

Thoroughly mix figs, gelatin and sugar in large saucepan. Bring to a boil over medium heat and continue boiling until figs are tender, about 3 minutes, stirring occasionally. Pour quickly into hot sterilized glasses. Cover at once with 1/8-inch hot paraffin. Cool and store in refrigerator. Makes 4 cups or 4 (8 fl. oz.) glasses.

Pastel Marshmallows

1 package (3 oz.) Jell-O brand gelatin, any flavor
1/2 cup boiling water
3/4 cup sugar
3 tablespoons light corn syrup
Confectioners sugar

Dissolve gelatin in boiling water in saucepan over very low heat. Add sugar. Cook and stir just until sugar is dissolved (do not boil). Blend in corn syrup. Chill until slightly thickened. Beat at highest speed of electric mixer (mixture is too stiff to be beaten by rotary beater) until mixture is thickened and will stand in soft peaks, about 8 to 10 minutes. Pour into 8- or 9-inch square pan which has been lined on sides and bottom with waxed paper greased with butter or margarine. Chill overnight.

Turn firm mixture out onto a board heavily dusted with confectioners sugar. Carefully peel off waxed paper and dust surfaces heavily with sugar. Cut into 1-inch squares or into shapes, using small cookie cutters dipped in sugar. Roll cut edges in sugar. Store tightly covered in refrigerator. Makes about 5 dozen confections.

The Gelatin Primer

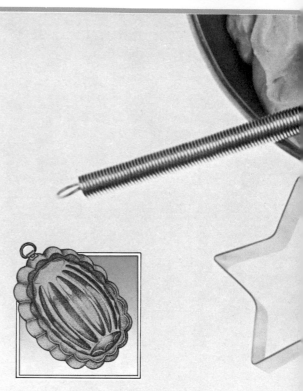

Making Jell-O gelatin is easy—you've probably been doing it since you were little. Just follow the package directions, and the results are terrific! In this primer you'll find tips to help ensure these terrific results, time after time. Find, too, special ways to help speed up gelatin setting when you're in a hurry. We also give you some quick ideas for varying your basic gelatin recipes, by adding flavor extras or by serving them in new and interesting ways—simple tricks that make dessert seem more special without a lot of work.

Move on to easy step-by-step instructions for molding gelatin—how to prepare it and how to unmold it for spectacular desserts and salads. And, finally, to clear up any questions you might have about just what is meant by certain terms used in recipes, there's a handy chart, on page 122, that spells out each stage of gelatin setting.

Just for Starters...

You'll follow the basic package or recipe directions, of course, but these extra tips will help, as well.

- To make a mixture that is clear and uniformly set, be sure the gelatin is *completely* dissolved in the boiling water or other liquid before adding the cold liquid.

- To make soft-set gelatin, increase the liquid about 1/2 cup for each 3 ounces of gelatin. The resulting dessert is softer, tastes delicious, but will be too soft to unmold.

- To double a recipe, just double the amounts of gelatin, liquid and other ingredients used, with the exception of salt, vinegar and lemon juice. For these, use just 1-1/2 times the amount called for.

- To make gelatin in a microwave oven, measure 1 cup water into a glass bowl. Place in oven and heat about 2 minutes, or until water comes to a boil. Remove from oven, add gelatin (3 oz. package) and stir until dissolved. Add 1 cup cold water and chill until set.

- To store prepared gelatin overnight or longer, cover it to prevent drying. Always store gelatin cakes or pies in the refrigerator.

If You're in a Hurry...

There are ways to speed up the chilling time, by choosing the right containers or using one of these specially developed speed sets.

The container you use can help hasten the setting. Use metal bowls or molds, rather than glass or china. Metal chills more quickly and the gelatin will be firm in less time than in glass bowls. Individual servings in small molds or serving dishes will also chill more quickly than large servings.

The ice cube way: Dissolve gelatin in boiling water as usual, then add 2 cups ice cubes (4 cups for 6 oz. package) and stir about 3 to 5 minutes to melt ice or until gelatin is thickened. Remove any unmelted ice. Gelatin will be soft-set in 30 minutes, firm in 1 to 1-1/2 hours. Do not use this method, however, if mixture is to be molded.

The blender method: Put gelatin (3 oz. package) and 3/4 cup boiling water in blender and blend at low speed until dissolved, about 1 minute. Add 1-1/2 cups crushed ice and blend at high speed until ice is melted, about 30 seconds. Pour into individual dishes or serving bowl and chill at least 30 minutes. Mixture is self-layering, with frothy layer on top, clear layer below.

The ice bath: Another way to hasten thickening of gelatin is to place the bowl of gelatin mixture in another bowl of ice and water; stir occasionally as mixture chills to ensure even thickening.

Now...the Extras

To add fruits or vegetables, chill gelatin until it is thickened, then fold in 3/4 to 1-1/2 cups (for 3 oz. package) of fresh or canned fruit or vegetables; if gelatin is not thick enough, the fruits or vegetables may float or sink. Do not use fresh or frozen pineapple, figs, mangoes or papayas; these fruits are fine, however, if cooked or canned. Canned or fresh fruit should be drained well before adding (unless recipe specifies otherwise); fruit juice or syrup can be used as part of the liquid called for.

Or add extra flavor these ways:

- Substitute carbonated soft drink for part or all of the water (if replacing boiling water, be sure to bring soft drink to a boil before dissolving gelatin). Use cola, ginger ale, root beer or any of the lemon- or lime-flavored mixes.
- Use fruit juice for all (boil, if replacing boiling water) or part of the liquid—orange juice, apple juice, cranberry juice, pineapple juice, etc.
- Add flavoring extracts—vanilla, almond, peppermint, for example, just a touch for a flavor plus.
- Add a little wine or liqueur for a festive touch—2 tablespoons of white wine, red wine, sherry or port, or 1 tablespoon creme de menthe or fruit-flavored liqueur.

Combine two flavors:

- For new flavor appeal, mix two Jell-O gelatin flavors—lemon or orange with any red flavor, for example, or any two red flavors.

No need to settle for gelatin in the same form every time. Try these different and easy ways with Jell-O gelatin!

Whip it! Chill prepared gelatin until very thick. Then beat with rotary beater or electric mixer until mixture is fluffy and thick and about double in volume; chill until firm. To shorten the chilling time, chill gelatin until slightly thickened, then use ice bath method, p. 116, and beat in bowl set in bowl of ice and water.

Flake it! Prepare gelatin as usual, reducing cold water to 3/4 cup (1-1/2 cups for 6 oz. package). Pour into shallow pan and chill until firm, at least 4 hours. Break into small flakes with a fork, or force through a ricer or large-mesh strainer. Pile lightly in dishes, alone or with fruit or topping.

Cube it! Prepare gelatin as usual, reducing cold water to 3/4 cup (1-1/2 cups for 6 oz. package). Pour into shallow pan and chill until firm, at least 4 hours or overnight. Cut in cubes, using sharp knife which has been dipped in hot water. To remove cubes from pan, apply warm wet cloth to bottom of pan, then remove with spatula. Or quickly dip pan in warm water and invert on waxed paper. Serve in glasses with cream or fruit, if desired.

Make cut-outs! Prepare gelatin as usual, reducing cold water to 1/2 cup (1 cup for 6 oz. package). Pour into 13x9-inch pan or to 1/4 inch depth in other shallow pans. Chill until firm. Cut designs, using cookie cutters that have been dipped in warm water. Transfer cut-outs to top of desserts, cakes, etc., using a broad spatula dipped in warm water. If only a few cut-outs are needed, flake remaining gelatin with a fork.

Layer it! Use for different flavors or different types of gelatin mixtures. Chill each layer until set, but not firm, before adding the next layer; if first layer is too firm, the layers may slip apart when unmolded. Except for the first layer, the gelatin mixtures should be cool and slightly thickened before being poured into mold; a warm mixture could soften the layer beneath it and cause mixtures to run together.

Tilt it! This is a different way of layering different flavors or mixtures. Prepare gelatin as usual. Fill small stemmed parfait, wine or sherbet glasses about half full. Tilt glasses in refrigerator by catching bases of glasses between bars of refrigerator rack and leaning tops of glasses against wall. Chill until set, but not firm, then add second mixture and chill until firm. Garnish with fruit, if desired.

Scallop it! Prepare gelatin as usual and pour into sherbet glasses. Chill until firm. Use 1/2-teaspoon measure to scoop out spoonfuls around edges, making scalloped borders. Top with whipped topping, filling scallops. Use scooped-out gelatin for garnish, if desired.

Molding How-To's

Gelatin desserts and salads look their most spectacular when molded. The making and the unmolding can be simple, if you follow these molding tips.

Use less water in preparing the gelatin mixture if dessert or salad is to be molded. For 3 ounce package of gelatin, use 3/4 cup cold water, for 6 ounce package, use 1-1/2 cups cold water. (This decrease has already been made in recipes in this book that are to be molded.) This makes the mold less fragile and makes unmolding much simpler.

As for the mold itself, almost any metal form, not necessarily the traditional mold, will work. If you have a collection of molds, that's fine. But if you lack them, consider using any of these less usual pans for molding, many of which have been used in recipes photographed in this book. Use cake pans—square 8- or 9-inch pans, round pans, fluted tube pans, tube pans or loaf cake or bread pans. Use metal mixing bowls; the nested sets give you a variety of sizes. Or use metal cans, from fruit or juices; to unmold, dip can in warm water, then puncture bottom of can and unmold.

Determine the volume of the mold first by measuring with water. Most recipes give an indication of the size mold needed. For clear gelatin, figure a 3 ounce package will make a little less than 2 cups, a 6 ounce package makes less than 4 cups. If mold holds less than the amount called for, the surplus might be poured into a separate dish for serving later. If the mold is much too big for the amount of gelatin mixture, it will be difficult to unmold and either the recipe should be increased or a smaller mold should be used.

To arrange fruits or vegetables in molds, chill gelatin until thick, then pour about 1/4 inch into mold. Arrange fruits or vegetables in a decorative pattern in the gelatin. Chill until set, but not firm, then pour remaining thickened gelatin over pattern in mold.

Now, the unmolding. First, allow gelatin to set until firm, several hours or overnight. Also, chill serving plate or individual plates on which mold will be served.
- Make certain that gelatin is completely firm. It should not feel sticky on top and should not sag toward the side if mold is tilted.
- Use a small pointed knife dipped in warm water to loosen top edge. Or, moisten tips of fingers and gently pull gelatin from edge of mold.
- Dip mold in warm, not hot, water, just to the rim, for about 10 seconds. Lift from water, hold upright and shake slightly to loosen gelatin. Or, gently pull gelatin from edge of mold.
- Moisten top of gelatin and the chilled serving plate with cold water; this allows gelatin to be moved after unmolding. Place moistened plate over mold and invert. Shake slightly, then lift off mold carefully. If gelatin doesn't release easily, dip the mold in warm water again. If necessary, move gelatin to center of serving plate.

1. Before unmolding, run knife around edge of gelatin. Or, pull gelatin from edge with moist fingers.

2. Dip mold in warm water, just to rim, for 10 seconds.

3. Lift from water and pull gelatin from edge of mold gently with moist fingers.

4. Place moistened serving plate on top of mold.

5. Invert mold and plate and shake to loosen gelatin.

6. Gently remove mold and center on plate.

Preparation Chart

When recipe says:	It means gelatin should…	It will take about: (regular set)	(speed set) Ice cube method not recommended for molding	Use it for…
"Chill until syrupy"	be consistency of thick syrup	1 hour	3 minutes	glaze for pies, fruits
"Chill until slightly thickened"	be consistency of unbeaten egg whites	1-1/4 hours	5 to 6 minutes	adding creamy ingredients like whipped topping or when mixture will be beaten
"Chill until thickened"	be thick enough so that spoon drawn through it leaves a definite impression	1-1/2 hours	5 to 6 minutes	adding solid ingredients like fruits or vegetables
"Chill until set but not firm"	stick to the finger when touched and should mound or move to the side when bowl or mold is tilted	2 hours	30 minutes	layering gelatin mixtures
"Chill until firm"	not stick to finger when touched and not mound or move when mold is tilted	individual molds: at least 3 hours 2- to 6-cup mold: at least 4 hours 8- to 12-cup mold: at least 5 hours or overnight	1 hour 2 hours	unmolding and serving

Angel Flake, Baker's, Birds Eye, Cool
Whip, Dream Whip, Good Seasons,
Jell-O and Maxwell House are
registered trademarks of General
Foods Corporation.

General Foods Consumer Center
250 North Street,
White Plains, New York 10625